teach®
yourself

PHP with MySQL

nat mcbride

teach®
yourself

PHP with MySQL

nat mcbride

for over 60 years, more than
50 million people have learnt over
750 subjects the **teach yourself**
way, with impressive results.

be where you want to be
with **teach yourself**

For UK order enquiries: please contact Bookpoint Ltd, 130 Milton Park, Abingdon, Oxon OX14 4SB. Telephone: +44 (0)1235 827720. Fax: +44 (0)1235 400454. Lines are open 09.00–17.00, Monday to Saturday, with a 24-hour message answering service. Details about our titles and how to order are available at www.teachyourself.co.uk.

For USA order enquiries: please contact McGraw-Hill Customer Services, PO Box 545, Blacklick, OH 43004-0545, USA. Telephone: 1-800-722-4726. Fax: 1-614-755-5645.

For Canada order enquiries: please contact McGraw-Hill Ryerson Ltd, 300 Water St, Whitby, Ontario L1N 9B6, Canada. Telephone: 905 430 5000. Fax: 905 430 5020.

Long renowned as the authoritative source for self-guided learning – with more than 50 million copies sold worldwide – the **teach yourself** series includes over 500 titles in the fields of languages, crafts, hobbies, business, computing and education.

British Library Cataloguing in Publication Data: a catalogue record for this title is available from The British Library.

Library of Congress Catalog Card Number: on file.

First published in UK 2005 by Hodder Education, 338 Euston Road, London, NW1 3BH.

First published in US 2005 by the McGraw-Hill Companies Inc.

The **teach yourself** name is a registered trademark of Hodder Headline.

 Typeset by MacDesign, Southampton

Printed in Great Britain for Hodder Education, a division of Hodder Headline, 338 Euston Road, London NW1 3BH, by Cox & Wyman Ltd, Reading, Berkshire.

Hodder Headline's policy is to use papers that are natural, renewable and recyclable products and made from wood grown in sustainable forests. The logging and manufacturing processes are expected to conform to the environmental regulations of the country of origin.

Impression number   10 9 8 7 6 5 4 3

Year   2009 2008 2007 2006

contents

	preface		viii
01	**introduction**		**1**
	1.1	Who this book is for	2
	1.2	Who this book is for (take two)	2
	1.3	What is PHP?	3
	1.4	What is MySQL?	5
	1.5	Why should you use PHP and MySQL?	5
	1.6	What can PHP do?	8
	1.7	Is it difficult?	9
	1.8	Help!	9
02	**getting started**		**11**
	2.1	What do you need to get started?	12
	2.2	How to install the Apache web server	15
	2.3	How to install PHP for use with Apache	18
	2.4	Configuring Apache and PHP to work together	21
	2.5	How to install PHP for use with Microsoft IIS	22
	2.6	Troubleshooting	24
	2.7	Your first PHP page	25
		Exercises	28
03	**PHP basics**		**29**
	3.1	Values and variables	30
	3.2	Variables in PHP	31
	3.3	Strings and numeric variables	33

3.4	Displaying information on a web page	35
3.5	Tying and cutting up strings	41
3.6	Maths lesson	43
3.7	Arrays	46
	Exercises	47
04	**statements and loops**	**49**
4.1	Control structures	50
4.2	If... Else...	52
4.3	While and Do... While...	60
4.4	For...	63
4.5	Foreach...	63
	Exercises	65
05	**talking to the browser**	**66**
5.1	Predefined variables	67
5.2	Getting information about the browser	67
5.3	Passing information using the URL	71
5.4	Your first (almost) dynamic page	73
	Exercises	78
06	**PHP for efficient HTML**	**80**
6.1	PHP for more efficient pages	81
6.2	Using included files	82
6.3	Using functions	90
	Exercises	95
07	**handling forms**	**97**
7.1	Using PHP to handle forms	98
7.2	Cleaning and validating data	101
7.3	Putting it all together	108
7.4	Displaying helpful error messages	111
	Exercises	115
08	**sessions and cookies**	**116**
8.1	Session variables and cookies	117
8.2	Using cookies	119
8.3	Using session variables	125
	Exercises	129

09	**installing MySQL**		**130**
	9.1	Downloading and installing MySQL	131
	9.2	Additional configuration for PHP	136
	9.3	Working with MySQL	137
10	**introduction to SQL**		**140**
	10.1	A brief overview of databases	141
	10.2	What is SQL?	143
	10.3	Creating a database with MySQL commands	144
	10.4	Working with database records	150
		Exercises	155
11	**using PHP with MySQL**		**157**
	11.1	Connecting to MySQL from a PHP page	158
	11.2	Extracting records from the database	160
	11.3	Putting data into the database	167
		Exercises	178
12	**converting ASP to PHP**		**179**
	12.1	Why change all my old code?	180
	12.2	About ASP2PHP	181
	12.3	Using ASP2PHP	184
	12.4	Some gotchas and 'what the …?'s	186
13	**reference section**		**189**
	13.1	Predefined variables	190
	13.2	Some common PHP operators	191
	13.3	Some common PHP functions	193
	13.4	Online resources	197
14	**answers to exercises**		**199**
	index		**213**

preface

So you've decided to get your head round PHP and MySQL? Good for you! You are joining one of the world's fastest-growing programming communities! From some humble beginnings a decade ago, PHP and MySQL have been recognized as equal or even superior to their expensive proprietary rivals for speed and power. The combination of PHP and MySQL is now the weapon of choice for thousands of web developers specializing in dynamic websites and applications. Whether you are looking at this technology as a career move, or to ensure that your sites are set on a sound, future-proofed technical footing, you have made the right decision.

I've been using PHP for about five years now and I just love it more and more. At first it was all a little intimidating – not because the language is hard (it isn't), but purely because of the lack of entry-level instruction. Everywhere I looked for help, it seemed to be written *by* techies *for* techies, and until you're up to speed with a technology, this can be really hard to follow.

The aim of this book is to give you a solid grounding and teach you enough to plan and build a dynamic website from the ground up. There are constant additions being made to the technology, so not even the fattest reference book can stay comprehensive for more than a couple of months. This book is part of the *Teach Yourself* series for a good reason – I firmly believe the best way to learn a new technology is to teach yourself by using it. Have a quick read through this book and decide on a pet project to learn PHP through. Then refer back to the book to guide you along the first few miles of your journey. Once you have the basics, you can confidently dip into online resources to find the most up-to-date advice on your particular needs.

Happy PHP-ing, you human dynamo, you!

Nat McBride, Southampton, 2005

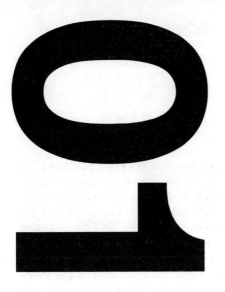

01

introduction

In this chapter you will learn:

- a little history of PHP and MySQL
- what makes PHP (and MySQL) so great
- who else uses these technologies instead of commercial rivals
- how easy it is to get started

1.1 Who this book is for

Before we go any further, let me just correct one common fallacy about PHP:

> **PHP is not just for teenage geeks.**

People who are not familiar with PHP – even some industry professionals – are often tempted to dismiss the technology as somehow amateurish, not suited to running serious commercial web services. They think it is only used by spotty youths in back bedrooms plotting to bring down Microsoft by playing *Half-Life* online. No. This is not true. Teenage geeks love PHP, grown-up geeks like me love PHP, but NASA and Amazon love PHP too. So do Mitsubishi, Volvo, Swatch, Infoseek, *Der Spiegel* and the W3C consortium, to name but a few of the high-profile organizations who use PHP themselves.

Now that we've cleared that up …

1.2 Who this book is for (take two)

Teach Yourself PHP and MySQL is an introduction to the PHP programming language. It assumes no prior knowledge of PHP or programming techniques, but does expect the reader to be familiar with HTML. You don't have to be a hand-coding HTML guru, but you should at least be able to look at the code snippets in this book and make sense of the HTML bits. If this isn't you, look back at the shelf where you got this book from – there should be a *Teach Yourself HTML* up there somewhere!

Since PHP is so often used in conjunction with a MySQL database, there are also a couple of chapters covering enough MySQL basics for you to be able to build a decent database-driven website. Again, no prior understanding of the technology is assumed – a lot of theory and science may go into creating super-efficient large-scale applications, but in fact you only need to understand the basics to create a good, solid database which will do the job you need it to.

PHP has similarities with other languages, notably C, C++ and Java, and this book may also be useful to programmers who already use these languages. If you just want to mug up on how certain principles are implemented in PHP, you may find this a handy reference. The basics of PHP will also be familiar to anyone who uses ASP/VBscript, though I must point out that with PHP you can go far beyond your wildest ASP dreams!

If you are any of the following, read on ...

- a student looking for an introduction to dynamic web technologies
- a web developer wanting to move from HTML into dynamic websites
- an ASP developer wanting to cross over into PHP
- any programmer wanting an introduction to PHP/MySQL
- a manager, IT strategist or consultant assessing the possibilities of PHP/MySQL.

1.3 What is PHP?

PHP is a server-side scripting language designed specifically for use with HTML to create more advanced web pages. It was originally developed for personal use in 1994 by a Danish software engineer called Rasmus Lerdorf. Lerdorf wanted some way of keeping track of who had been visiting his personal home page, so he built himself a set of tools using another server-side language, Perl. His visitors were interested in what he was doing, so he developed the tools into a kit (Personal Home Page Tools, hence PHP) which he made freely available to other people. This grew and incorporated new tools, and by 1997, there were 50,000 websites using PHP version 2.

Whose side are you on?

Web languages can be divided into two categories: 'client-side' and 'server-side'. 'Client-side' code is processed by the client machine – i.e. the computer being used by whoever is visiting the web page. HTML is a client-side language, which is handled by the user's web browser. 'Server-side' code is handled by the web server which hosts the page. When a user visits a page with server-side code in it, the server processes all the instructions and then sends the output as static HTML code to the user's browser.

At this point it still wasn't really a language as such – just a collection of useful tools and functions – Lerdorf describes himself as a 'techy adept at solving problems' rather than a programmer. There was however an active community of developers working with Lerdorf in the collaborative, open-source manner to extend PHP's capabilities. In 1997 two Israeli programmers, Zeev Suraski and Andi Gutmans, hit some frustrating limitations, and decided to give it a thorough overhaul. They rewrote many crucial modules to increase its flexibility; PHP3 was released with these changes incorporated, and its popularity soared.

PHP4 was released in June 2000, with significant changes to the structure and security of the previous version. Several interim versions were released over the following four years, and the current version 5 came out in July 2004. It is generally considered to be a mature language now, which will continue to develop but won't radically alter in the near future. With over 500 talented developers putting their love and free time into the PHP project, it is never going to stand still – but if you've been hesitant about getting involved with PHP before, you certainly don't need to be any more.

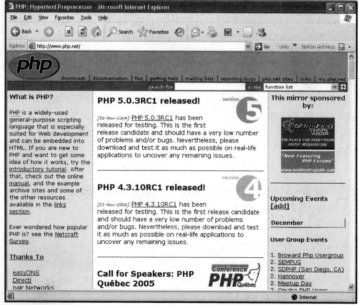

www.php.net – the official PHP website, for downloads, documentation, etc.

Incidentally, to reflect the fact that it has come a long way since the early days of Personal Home Page tools, PHP now stands for PHP: Hypertext Preprocessor.

1.4 What is MySQL?

The development of MySQL ('My Ess Queue Ell') began with a Swedish IT company called TcX. In 1979 a programmer there, Monty Widenius, wrote a piece of software to work with raw data. He expanded this over the next 15 years, but by 1994 the volumes of data it had to handle were just getting too much for it. Widenius and TcX looked around for a replacement and found a small but efficient database application called Hughes mSQL, developed by David Hughes. mSQL didn't have all the features they needed to handle large data stores either, so Widenius took the basic model and souped it up, creating MySQL in 1995.

SQwhat?

Structured Query Language is a common language under-stood by all relational databases. It is used alongside other languages such as PHP (or ASP, Perl, Java, etc.) to talk to a database, to read or write data to it.

The first version of MySQL did not aim to compete with big database applications like Oracle, but in the 10 years since then, it has developed a raft of comparable features. The current stable release is 4.1, with MySQL 5.0 in production now. It is certainly a rival to any other database, and is substantially more cost-effective.

1.5 Why should you use PHP and MySQL?

Because it's easy to learn, it's as good as or better than the alternatives, and much cheaper. Generally free, in fact.

What, you need more reasons? OK, let's expand on those three points.

It's easy to learn

PHP uses an intuitive syntax, so even if you've never had any formal computer science training, you will get to grips with the rudiments of programming very quickly. There's a predefined function for pretty much anything you could wish for, so you can perform complicated functions without writing complicated code.

With some languages, there are real hurdles to getting started – for instance, you often need to understand quite a lot of scary-looking theory about variable types and scope before you can do anything. PHP simplifies the use of variables so you can dive right into the business of making stuff happen.

It's as good as anything else, or better

You can write very simple scripts very easily with PHP, but the more you learn, the more you can extend your powers without outgrowing the language. PHP is extremely comprehensive, and is compatible with a huge range of platforms, servers and databases.

And it's not just big, it's clever. The PHP source code is tested by a wide and expanding community of developers. These people do not get paid for their work, there are no 'jobsworths' involved, no managers with a personal incentive to bury bad news. The developers' reward is recognition by their peers, which comes through finding and fixing bugs, and improving existing features.

For those of you who are coming to PHP from other languages, version 5 of PHP now properly supports object-oriented programming, although there is no space to cover it in this book.

It's free (nearly always)

PHP is an entirely open-source project which is free to download and use. MySQL is developed as a commercial product, but the terms of its licence are very open – for most purposes, you can use MySQL under a free open-source licence. If you are developing a website (even if you intend to make money out of the site by selling goods or services), you don't have to pay for MySQL. You only need to pay for a commercial licence if you use MySQL to develop software which you then sell on to your own customers as a licensed application.

The bottom line

PHP and MySQL are in my opinion the only way to go – but you don't have to take my word for it, just look at the numbers. At the time of writing, there were over 5 million MySQL installations across the Web, and almost 18.5 million websites using PHP! According to TIOBE, a coding standards company that runs a regular survey of different programming languages, PHP is the fourth most popular language, and rising fast. And as I mentioned above, the organizations using PHP are not just small eccentric outfits, they include large blue-chip companies.

If you want to check today's usage figures, try the following links:

PHP usage: www.php.net/usage.php

MySQL usage: www.mysql.com/company/factsheet.html

PHP popularity: www.tiobe.com/tpci.htm

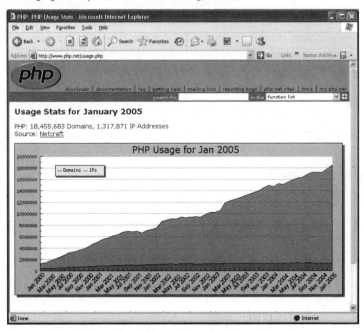

18,455,683 websites using PHP… and counting!

1.6 What can PHP do?

- **Web pages.** PHP is used first and foremost as server-side scripting for creating rich interactive web pages.

- **Web applications.** It can also be used to write web applications which never actually reach a browser window. For instance, I have a PHP script on one of my sites which handles notifications from PayPal about credit card transactions. No browser is involved in this at all – the PayPal server sends an HTTP request to the server hosting my site, which uses the PHP script to confirm the transaction and then store the information in a sales database.

- **Command line scripting.** PHP can also be used from the command prompt of your operating system. For the average individual user this is of little interest, but it is very handy for server administrators who can write time-saving scripts for regular maintenance tasks, for instance.

- **Desktop applications.** To write desktop applications using PHP, you need to get an extension to the main PHP download, called PHP-GTK. This is not a common use of PHP, but it is sometimes done to create windowed applications which work on any platform – because they are powered by PHP rather than any specific operating system.

Server-side scripting

It is important to appreciate the consequences of server-side scripting for interactivity. PHP code is executed at the server, unlike Javascript or Flash scripting, which is handled locally by the user's browser and associated plug-ins. If you call for some kind of user input, it must be sent via the browser back to the server, processed, and the result then sent from the server back to the browser. This may not have an obvious impact when developing code on your development machine, where both client and server are installed. But when you take it into a live environment, delivering pages over the Internet, every additional fraction of a second becomes important.

PHP is not for designing games or other web applications where there is a need for fast, high-volume, continuous input from the user. That isn't to say you can't use PHP to build an online game – but think strategy, not real-time action.

1.7 Is it difficult?

No, it really isn't. There's a lovely shallow learning curve to PHP which means you can get started with a tiny scraping of knowledge and gradually build up your skills. It's not one of those things which call for a heavy up-front investment in learning lots of theory before you can achieve anything. MySQL is much the same – you can make a fairly complex database-driven site without knowing more than a few basic SQL commands. In both cases, you'll find that with time and practice you discover much better ways of doing things, and will probably end up re-writing much of your early work – but so what? The early stuff may not be as efficient as it could be, but in the mean time, you have been building functional, effective dynamic websites, and learning valuable real-world lessons along the way.

In fact, probably the trickiest thing about PHP is getting yourself a development environment set up. Before you can start playing around with code, you need to download and install a web server and the PHP source code. But even this isn't so hard these days: there are self-installing versions of both which need only minor configuring, and you can also find packages which bundle up PHP with a web server and database, all pre-configured and pretty much ready to go. We'll cover installation issues in detail in the next chapter.

1.8 Help!

And once you get up and running, you can be sure you're not alone. The open-source nature of PHP development means that there are a vast number of PHP experts out there who are all committed to a collaborative way of using and sharing knowledge. No matter how obscure your query, there will be someone who has had the same problem before and found a solution.

The downside to this is that experts are often not very good at explaining things to non-experts. I would recommend getting yourself up to speed with the basics before you try digging into the official PHP manual. It's detailed, accurate and has real-world examples contributed by readers – but it's definitely not for the absolute beginner!

OK … got that then? Don't worry, all will become clear …

But the point is this: if you're ever out of your depth and get stuck, you will find plenty of people online who are willing and able to help out – even if you do have to refer to this and other books to understand their advice!

Summary

- PHP is a powerful and flexible server-side web scripting language.

- MySQL is a relational database management system suitable for all web applications, including high-end use.

- Both PHP and MySQL are generally used under a no-cost open source licence agreement.

- Together, they are used by major government and commercial organisations to create interactive websites.

- Though rich enough to support complex web applications, PHP and MySQL are also very beginner-friendly.

02 getting started

In this chapter you will learn:

- where to get the software you need to run PHP

- how to install a web server

- how to install PHP

- how to configure them to work together

- how to write your first PHP page

2.1 What do you need to get started?

To serve up PHP pages, you need two pieces of software which you probably don't already have on your computer: a web server and the PHP engine. Premium editions of Windows (Windows XP Professional/Enterprise/etc.) have their own web server called IIS – Internet Information Services. This may or may not have been installed yet, but you will be able to do so from your Windows CD by following the normal steps for adding Windows components. Then you can just install PHP and configure accordingly (more on this on page 22 below).

You can run PHP on any operating system – Windows, Mac OS or Linux – but I'm assuming (sorry) that most readers are working on Windows, so will start from there. I'm also assuming that most readers are using a non-premium edition of Windows and will need to install a web server too. The most common choice is the Apache web server, which is another piece of open-source software. It's free, safe and reliable – according to a recent Netcraft survey, more than 67% of all web sites use Apache.

WAMP

If you're feeling the need for another acronym at this point, you're in luck – this combination of Windows-Apache-MySQL-PHP is commonly known as WAMP.

We won't actually need to install MySQL until later in the book, so to keep things simple, the following pages only explain how to install and configure Apache and PHP. If you want to install MySQL as well now, slip a bookmark into page 131 and refer to that once you have the first two installed.

Not a Windows user?

If you have a Mac OS X (10.1 or above), there should be a version of the Apache web server and PHP pre-installed – all you have to do is activate it. There is a nice straightforward tutorial at www.sanbeiji.com/tech/tutorials/php/index.php

For detailed instructions on downloading and installing on a Mac, try http://phpmac.com (be warned – you must not be afraid of using the command line!).

If you are a Linux user, you probably already have PHP pre-installed. If not, you are spoilt for choice in terms of installation help – run a search for "installation tutorial LAMP" (Linux-Apache-MySQL-PHP) and you will find umpteen handy guides to take you through the process.

Downloads

First of all, you will need to get your hands on the software. Follow the links below to download Apache and PHP.

1   Go to http://httpd.apache.org/download.cgi and find the section headed **Apache 2.0.52 is the best available version** (the version number may be different by the time you read this).

2   Find the link to the **Win32 Binary (MSI Installer)**, right-click and choose **Save Target As...**, and save the file somewhere on your computer.

3   If you want to verify that the download is the genuine article (recommended), you should do the same with the **MD5** link – but save it as *apache-md5.txt* instead of the filename it suggests. We'll deal with verification in the next section.

4   Now go to http://www.php.net/downloads.php and scroll down to the section headed **PHP 5.0.2** (again, the version number may have changed since the time of writing).

5   Find the link to the **PHP 5.0.2 Installer**. Copy the MD5 number if you want to verify your download, and paste into a text file, then save it.

6   Follow the **PHP 5.0.2 Installer** link, and select a download mirror. Right-click and save the file.

Verifying the software

It is at least 99.99% safe to download and install software if you get it from the official PHP and Apache sites. Apparently, Apache was briefly cracked a couple of years ago but no downloads were affected. However, it is good practice to verify the files you download before you install them, (a) just in case, and (b) because if crackers know that most people will verify downloads, there's no point them wasting their time trying to get you to download a dodgy version.

Verification is not essential, but it doesn't take long and will give you that extra peace of mind. There are two ways to verify that a download is the genuine article; we'll use a thing called an MD5 checksum. A checksum is a hexadecimal number created by applying an algorithm to the contents of the entire file – it'll look something like this: f53c7a0cdd1a6c63ad74316d4e82cf4f.

The Apache or PHP developers run the MD5 algorithm on their official software releases, and publish the resulting number. You then download what you hope is a genuine copy, run the MD5 algorithm yourself, and compare the results. If the two match, you know you've got the real thing. To do the comparison, you'll need a little MD5 program.

Checking with MD5

1   Go to the Solid Blue website http://winmd5sum.solidblue.biz and scroll to the **Download winMd5Sum** link. Click to run the installer and follow the instructions.

2   You should now find a new program on your Start menu – go to **winMd5Sum** and run it. A small program window will open.

3   Click the **...** button next to the **File name input** and browse to find and select your downloaded file.

4   **winMd5Sum** should now display the filename and the checksum generated from it.

5   Now dig out the MD5 number you saved when downloading the file. Copy and paste it into the **Compare** input, then click **Compare**.

2.2 How to install the Apache web server

Now that you have your Apache download and you know that it's the genuine article, you're ready to install it. Browse to the download and double-click to run the installer.

When prompted for network domain and server name, enter 'localhost'. I'm assuming that at this early stage in your PHP career, you just want to use the web server for your own development work, not to make it publicly available across the Internet! Enter anything for the administrator's e-mail address – this is only really applicable to publicly-accessed servers.

On the next screen, select the **Typical setup** type, and on the next screen, choose a location to install the server (I'd leave it as the default unless you have a good reason not to). Now click **Install**.

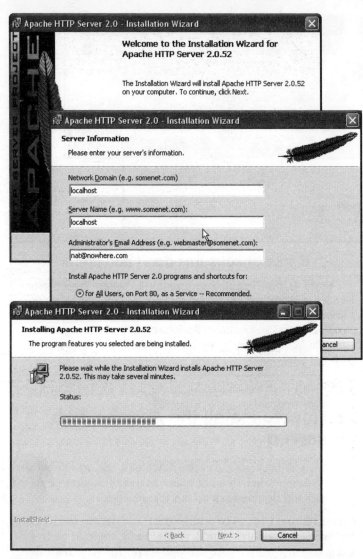

Working through the Apache installation wizard

As the files are installed, you should notice a couple of command prompt windows popping up and then disappearing again. If you have a Windows firewall, you may find that it tries to block some parts of the program – click **Unblock** to prevent it from interfering with the server.

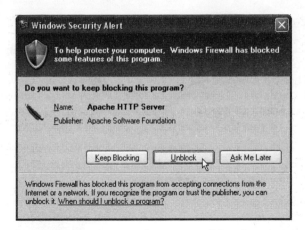

When the installation is complete you will be shown a success message, and you should also now see a little Apache icon on the task bar to show that it is installed and running. If you click this, a menu appears allowing you to stop, start or restart the server.

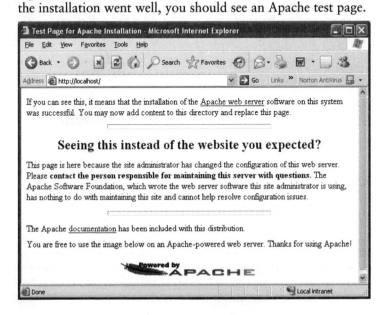

Open a browser and type **http://localhost** into the address bar. If the installation went well, you should see an Apache test page.

If you can see this, it means that the installation of the Apache web server software on this system was successful. You may now add content to this directory and replace this page.

Seeing this instead of the website you expected?

This page is here because the site administrator has changed the configuration of this web server. Please **contact the person responsible for maintaining this server with questions.** The Apache Software Foundation, which wrote the web server software this site administrator is using, has nothing to do with maintaining this site and cannot help resolve configuration issues.

The Apache documentation has been included with this distribution.

You are free to use the image below on an Apache-powered web server. Thanks for using Apache!

File locations

By default, Apache sets the directory **C:\Program Files\Apache Group\Apache2\htdocs** as the 'document root'. This is where Apache will look for web files when you point your browser at http://localhost/. If you want to keep your web files elsewhere, you will need to configure Apache accordingly. To change the location of your document root:

1 From the Windows **Start** menu, choose **All Programs > Apache HTTP Server 2.0.52 > Configure Apache Server > Edit the Apache httpd.conf Configuration File.**

2 This will open the config file in Notepad. Search for the term 'DocumentRoot' and edit the following lines with the appropriate directories.

```
DocumentRoot "C:/Program Files/Apache Group/
Apache2/htdocs"

<Directory "C:/Program Files/Apache Group/
Apache2/htdocs">
```

3 Both directories must be the same – and don't add a final slash to the path! Now save the file and close it.

4 To make the changes take effect, you must restart Apache: click the **Apache** icon, then choose **Apache2 > Restart.**

If you try the http://localhost/ test again now, you will either see the file called *index.html* (if you have one), or a file/directory listing.

2.3 How to install PHP for use with Apache

Before installing PHP, you should stop your web server if it is running – click the **Apache** icon, then choose **Apache > Stop.** Find the PHP download and double-click to run the installer.

When prompted, choose the Standard installation, and (unless you have a good reason), accept the default directory of C:\PHP. On the next page, leave the SMTP server name and 'from' e-mail address as the defaults – again, this really only applies to a public server.

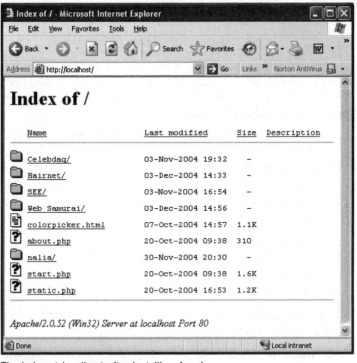

The index at localhost after installing Apache

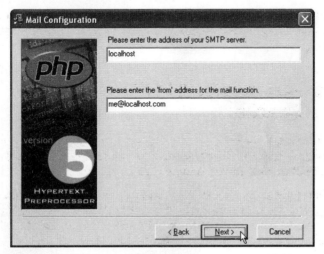

Starting to install PHP for use with Apache

Next, select the server type: **Apache**.

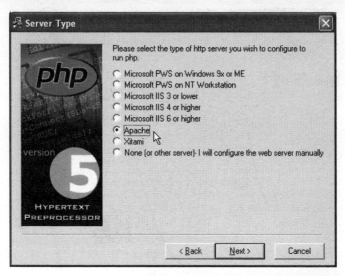

The installer now has all it needs to set up PHP, so click **Next** to install.

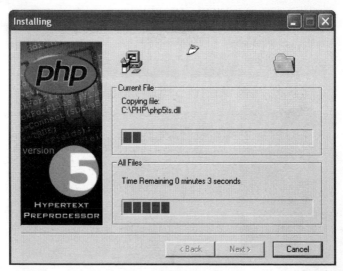

2.4 Configuring Apache and PHP to work together

Unless those nice people at the PHP group have upgraded the Windows installer since the time of writing, you will probably see this message when you complete the PHP install:

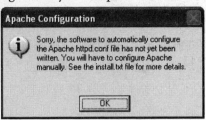

Apache Configuration

Sorry, the software to automatically configure the Apache httpd.conf file has not yet been written. You will have to configure Apache manually. See the install.txt file for more details.

OK

But it's OK – manual configuration is pretty easy. Here is what you need to do:

1 Go to the Windows folder (C:\Windows or C:\WinNT) and open the php.ini file in Notepad or another text editor.

2 Search for the term 'doc_root' and edit the following line so that it matches the document root you set while installing Apache:

```
doc_root = "C:/Program Files/Apache Group/
Apache2/htdocs"
```

3 Save and close the file.

4 Open the Apache **httpd.conf** file again (see above).

5 Scroll down to the end of the file and add the following lines:

```
ScriptAlias /php/ "c:/php/"
AddType application/x-httpd-php .php
Action application/x-httpd-php "/php/php-cgi.exe"
```

6 Save and close the file, and start up the Apache server.

To test that Apache and PHP are now both happily installed and talking to each other, open a blank text file and type this line:

```
<? phpinfo(); ?>
```

Save this in your document root directory as **test.php**. Now point your browser at **http://localhost/test.php** – if you see a page like the one overleaf, congratulations – you are ready to start coding!

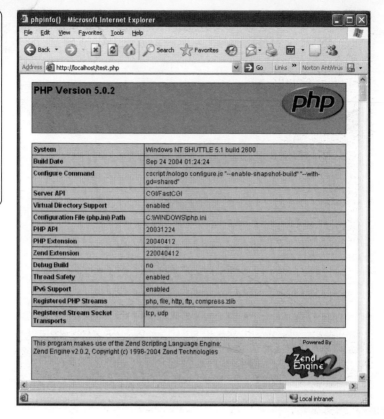

2.5 How to install PHP for use with Microsoft IIS

If you are going to use Microsoft's web server, the installer will do most of the configuration itself. Browse to your PHP download file and double-click to run it.

When prompted, choose the **Standard** installation, and (unless you have a good reason), accept the default directory of **C:\PHP**.

On the next page, leave the SMTP server name and 'from' e-mail address as the defaults – again, this really only applies to a public server.

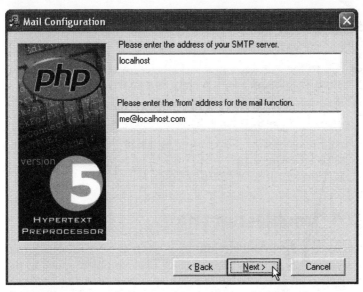

Next, select the appropriate version of **Microsoft IIS** as the server type.

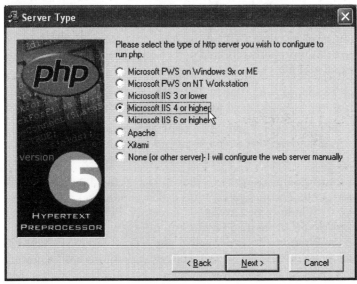

The installer now has all it needs to set up PHP, so click **Next** to install.

You now have one final configuration step, related to a security feature of PHP which is enabled by default but is not needed for IIS.

1   Go to the Windows folder (**C:\Windows** or **C:\WinNT**) and open the **php.ini** file in Notepad or some other text editor.

2   Search for the term **cgi.force_redirect** and check that it is set to 0. If it is not, change it to 0 and save the file.

For more details, or if you want to install PHP with IIS manually, the following article is helpful: http://www.macromedia.com/devnet/mx/dreamweaver/articles/php_iis.html

2.6 Troubleshooting

If you don't get the PHP info page when you try to view http://localhost/test.php, go back over the lines you have added to the Apache and PHP configuration files. The most likely explanation is a small typo, or a directory path that doesn't quite match up with the actual location.

Use Windows Explorer to check that the paths you have entered to your document root and to the **php-cgi.exe** file are right. If you have installed PHP somewhere other than **C:/PHP**, make sure this is properly reflected in the **ScriptAlias** line in the Apache **httpd.conf** file.

Let's suppose you installed PHP to **F:/MyPrograms/PHP**. In this case, the lines you need to add to httpd.conf will be:

```
ScriptAlias /php/ "f:/myprograms/php/"
AddType application/x-httpd-php.php
Action application/x-httpd-php "/php/php-cgi.exe"
```

Another possible problem is that you have edited the wrong PHP config file. The one you want is called **php.ini** and it is found in the C:\Windows or C:\WinNT directory. PHP stores a backup copy of this file in the PHP/Backup directory, and also saves one in the Windows directory called **php.bak.ini**. You may have edited these by mistake – check and try again if this has happened.

> ### Installing MySQL
>
> You don't need MySQL for the first few chapters of this book, but if you want to get all the fiddly installation jobs out of the way now, skip ahead to page 131 and install MySQL as well.

2.7 Your first PHP page

Ready? Excited? I have some good news and some bad news for you. The bad news is that you've already written your first PHP page, the **test.php** file we used above. This is probably a bit of an anti-climax, but the good news is – it really is that easy!

Well OK, that one doesn't really count anyway. Let's write some proper PHP. Type the following into a text file and save it in your document root directory as **helloworld.php**:

```
<?
echo "Hello world!" ;
?>
```

Now view it in your browser. Nothing very special there – you could have done the same thing in HTML without all the weird question marks and 'echoing'. But now try viewing the source code for the page, using the browser (i.e. choose **View Source** from the menu). Notice that there is no PHP code visible – all you get is `Hello world!`

This is because no PHP code *ever* reaches the browser. The web server, together with the PHP engine, processes any PHP instructions and sends the resulting (static) output to the browser. If you're used to working with client-side code like HTML or Javascript, this is worth understanding properly before we go any further.

What happens to PHP code?

First of all, the web server is primed to expect PHP code because the file we requested has the extension **.php**. This activates the PHP engine to scan through the file and look for any instructions it needs to process. The angle brackets and question marks (`<?` and `?>`) denote a block of PHP code – any code not enclosed by these markers will be ignored. Instructions are separated by semi-colons at the end of lines.

In our example, there is just one PHP instruction: **echo**. This is a very common PHP function used to output information to the browser. Anything in quotes (double or single) following the **echo** function is treated as output destined for the browser. The web server then parcels up the PHP output (along with any ordinary HTML code) and sends the result as a web page for the browser to display.

Embedding PHP in HTML

Since most PHP is used in a web context, the chances are you will not be coding exclusively in PHP – you will use it together with HTML. As the process outlined above suggests, you can mix and match your code to your heart's content, as long as each block of PHP is clearly marked out.

So for instance, we can take our 'Hello world!' script and re-write it as follows to produce the same output:

```
<HTML>
<BODY>
Hello <? echo "world!" ; ?>
</BODY>
</HTML>
```

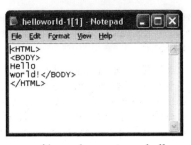

Type this into a text file and save it as **helloworld-1.php,** and view it in your browser. Take a look at the source for this page – all that is left is the HTML code plus the *output* from the PHP code, which is spliced into the HTML at the point where the original PHP code went. To see this in action even more clearly, try the following:

```
<HTML>
<BODY>
Hel<? echo "lo" ; ?> wo<? echo "rld!" ; ?>
</BODY>
</HTML>
```

The resulting page and page source are exactly the same as in the last example. And the output is not limited to displaying text on the screen – you can use PHP to write HTML tags too. Try this:

```
<HTML>
<BODY>
Hello
<? echo "<b>" ; ?>world!<? echo "</b>" ; ?>
</BODY>
</HTML>
```

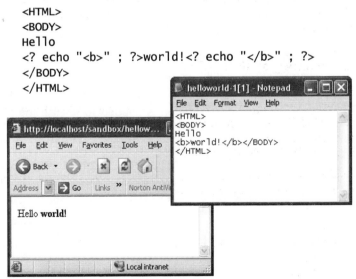

Of course, there's not much point using all that extra code just to write plain HTML tags, but it is powerful when combined with other PHP functions, as we will start to see in the next chapter.

Exercises

1   Use WinMd5Sum to calculate the checksum for a Word document on your computer. Now open the document, change one letter and re-save it. Run the checksum again and compare the results.

2   Write a page using a mixture of PHP and HTML to produce the following output in a web browser:

I am a **bold** adventurer into the world of *PHP programming*.

Remember to save the file with a **.php** extension.

3   Use PHP embedded into the <BODY> tag to make the page background your favourite colour.

Summary

+   **PHP can be downloaded from www.php.net, and the Apache web server is available at www.apache.org.**

+   **MD5 checksums are used to verify that you have authentic versions of the software.**

+   **Installation is mainly handled by the installers which come with PHP and Apache.**

+   **Some manual configuration is needed to finalize the settings and get PHP and Apache working together.**

+   **PHP code is read and executed by the web server, which then sends plain HTML output to the browser for display.**

+   **PHP can be embedded anywhere in an HTML page, as long as it is marked as such by the <? and ?> tags.**

03

PHP basics

In this chapter you will learn:

- about values and variables, strings, numbers and arrays
- how to use variables to display information on the page
- how to manipulate pieces of text
- how to perform mathematical calculations

3.1 Values and variables

If you have not worked with other programming languages, it is worth taking a few minutes to get to grips with some basic concepts. A *variable* is a bit like the joker in a deck of cards – it has no fixed value (hence 'variable'). Instead, it can be assigned a value by its user. The ace of spades is always the ace of spades and the four of diamonds is always the four of diamonds. But a joker may have the value of any card at any given time – it may even change its value over the course of a game.

Similarly, if you write height="50" in the <img> tag of an HTML page, that image will always be 50 pixels high. But if you were to replace the constant number 50 with a variable, you could then assign whatever value you liked to it. The value could also be determined from a series of calculations which your PHP script performs.

You could also change the contents of the image's alt attribute – a variable does not have to have a numeric value. If you write alt="Red wins" in your code, then the image's alt text will always read "Red wins". But if you replace it with a variable, it could be changed according to other factors which your script deals with.

You can see from these examples that you could use variables as the basis of a voting script which displays the results of user votes on a bar graph. Imagine if you could only use HTML to show the results of a popularity vote between Red team and Blue team. You would have to code thousands of pages with different combinations of red and blue bars of different sizes, some with the text "Red wins" and "Blue loses" in the alt tags, and some with "Red loses" and "Blue wins". And then you would have to count up the votes yourself and determine which file to display when the results page is requested. Impossible!

Using PHP to manipulate the values of variables, a single file becomes flexible enough to display a results page with the correct image sizes and alt text.

Variables are the bread and butter of all programming – the whole point of any program is to take a set of unknown inputs and process them to produce some other output.

Constants

It is also possible to define constants in PHP, which are like variables except that once they are defined, they cannot be changed later on in your script. It is not used very often, because there isn't much point – it's easier to define a variable than a constant, and you never know, it might be useful at some point in the future to be able to modify its value.

3.2 Variables in PHP

You will recognize a PHP variable by its dollar prefix:

```
$variable
```

This tells the PHP parser 'this next bit is a variable – don't take it literally, and don't try to interpret it as a command'. Suppose you were to write a line of PHP like this:

```
I can hear an <? echo echo ; ?>
```

PHP would look at this and throw an error, because it looks like you're trying to use the echo function twice, without telling it what to output.

Now suppose you did the same sort of thing but the second word was not a recognized PHP function:

```
I like <? echo cheese ; ?>
```

PHP would look at this and decide that 'cheese' is some kind of constant. Put this line into an HTML page and view it in a browser. If you have not changed the default error reporting options in the PHP configuration file, you should see a message like this:

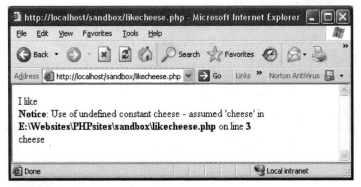

This is not a serious enough error to cause the page to fail completely, but you do get an error notice telling you that you have not defined this constant 'cheese'. It also tells you that the parser has assumed you wanted to give the constant the value 'cheese', and displayed that value after the error message.

However, if we try the same trick but this time we mark 'cheese' as being a variable with the dollar sign, we get a different result:

```
I like <? echo $cheese ; ?>
```

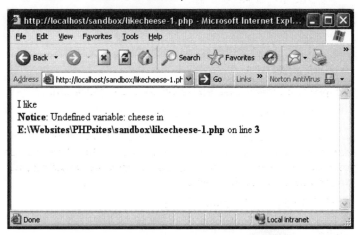

As before, we get an error notice telling us we have not defined the variable 'cheese'. Only this time, because PHP knows that 'cheese' is a variable, it is not a good idea to assume anything about its value, so it doesn't give it a value at all.

Defining variables

Defining variables in PHP couldn't be easier. We simply think up a variable name, and use the equals sign to give it a value. So for example:

```
<? $cheese = "cheddar" ; ?>
I like <? echo $cheese ; ?>
```

The output of this will be displayed in the browser:

```
I like cheddar.
```

Variable rules

There are a few rules which must be followed when giving variables names.

* They can include letters, numbers and underscores but not spaces.

    `$kind_of_cheese` is OK

    `$kind of cheese` is not

* They must not start with a number.

    `$cheese1` is OK

    `$1stcheese` is not

* Upper and lower case letters are different characters.

    `$STILTON` is not the same as `$stilton`

A variable can be redefined at any point in your script, just by using the equals sign again to assign it a new value. At any given point in the script, the variable holds the value most recently assigned to it. So the following ...

```
<? $cheese = "cheddar" ; ?>
I like <? echo $cheese ; ?>
<br/>
<? $cheese = "stilton" ; ?>
I also like <? echo $cheese ; ?>
```

... will produce this result:

```
I like cheddar
I also like stilton
```

3.3 Strings and numeric variables

Variables do not only have values, they also have 'types' which determine what kind of value it can have. If the variable is a string type, it has a text value such as "gorgonzola" or "hello, this is a message from number 11". A string is literally just a string of characters with no intrinsic meaning. If the variable is a numeric type, its value is a number which can be operated on by mathematical functions.

In most programming languages you have to define the variable type, and if you want to change its type once it has been defined, you need to do so explicitly. So if the variable $cheese had been defined as "57", you could not simply take that variable and add 1 to it to make 58. You would first have to tell the parser 'actually, I changed my mind – I want $cheese to be a number now, the number 57'.

PHP is much more forgiving – the variable type may change throughout your script depending on its context. PHP looks at the way you are trying to use a variable and assigns or changes its type automatically. Suppose for instance you have a variable $num. You can give it the value 10 using either of the following constructions:

```
$num = "10" ;
$num = 10 ;
```

In the first, the quotes imply that "10" is a string to be used for textual purposes. In the second, you are implying that the number 10 is to be used mathematically. But in PHP it doesn't matter which way you do it, because the variable type will be automatically changed for each purpose. If you try to perform a mathematical operation on $num – adding 5 to it, for instance – then the parser will treat it as a numeric variable and return the number 15. If you try to perform a string function on it – sticking it together with other strings such as "I am " and " years old", then the parser will treat it as a string, and return the string "I am 10 years old".

When you assign a text value to a variable, you must enclose it in quotes so that the parser reads it literally and does not try to interpret the text as PHP instructions.

Other variable types

In fact, there are other types of variable: integers, floating point values (decimal numbers), strings, Boolean (true/false), NULL, arrays, objects and resources. We will come across some of these later in the book, but stick to the simple distinction between numbers and strings for now.

3.4 Displaying information on a web page

We have been using the PHP function echo to send text or variables to the browser. When sending plain text as in the 'Hello world!' example, we enclosed the text in quotes. When using it with variables as in the cheese example, we dispensed with the quotes. In fact, there are several ways in which echo can be used, all of which are equally effective.

```
<?
echo "Using double quotes <br/>" ;
echo 'Using single quotes <br/>' ;
$sometext = "Using a variable <br/>" ;
echo $sometext ;
?>
```

Which gives the output:

```
Using double quotes
Using single quotes
Using a variable
```

We can also combine plain text and variables in the same echo statement, but if we want the value of the variable to be output, we must use double quotes, not single. For instance, try viewing the following in a browser:

```
<?
$sometext = "variable" ;
echo "Using double quotes and a $sometext <br/>" ;
echo 'Using single quotes and a $sometext <br/>' ;
?>
```

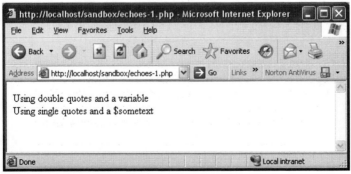

When using echo with single quotes, the variable is read literally, as if it were an ordinary string. With double quotes, the parser keeps an eye out for any variables marked with the dollar sign and outputs their value instead.

Escape characters

What if we wanted to include quotation marks in the output though? Well, we could get away with something like this:

```
echo 'Using single quotes to "display" double
quotes' ;
echo "Using double quotes to 'display' single
quotes" ;
```

But what if the sentence also had an apostrophe to display?

```
echo "This isn't going to "work", is it?" ;
```

When the parser gets to the double quote at the beginning of "work", it thinks it has reached the end of the expected output because you have closed the opening double quote. It knows it should return "This isn't going to ", but it doesn't know what to do with the rest of the line, so it throws an error.

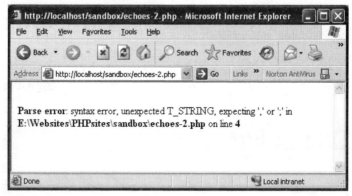

Using single quotes instead of double won't solve the problem:

```
echo 'And this won't "work" either!' ;
```

Likewise, when the parser reaches the apostrophe in "won't", you have closed the opening single quote, and will get as far as 'And this won' before getting stuck again.

We can tell the parser to ignore characters like quotes which have special programmatic meanings, by using another one with a special meaning, called an escape character. The escape character in PHP is a backslash (\), and it tells the parser 'don't try to interpret the character immediately after this one – just read it literally'. So to produce some output with a mixture of single and double quotes, we could do this:

```
echo "I'm glad we can use \"escape characters\"!
<br/>" ;
```

Notice that we do not escape the single quote in "I'm". This is because the echo statement has been opened with a double quote, so in this context only another double quote character has any special meaning. We could produce the same output using single quotes like this:

```
echo 'I\'m glad we can use "escape characters"!
<br/>' ;
```

In this case it's the single quote which needs to be escaped, and the doubles are fine. If you want to output the backslash too, you escape it in exactly the same way, by putting one backslash in front of another:

```
echo "We can even escape the \\ if we want." ;
```

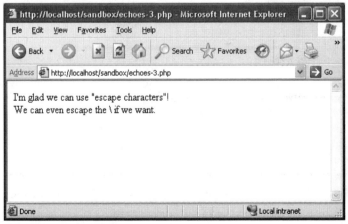

Outputting HTML

We already know that it is possible to use echo to return HTML code in exactly the same way as text displayed on the page – we have included line breaks and bold formatting tags in previous examples. There is however a small disadvantage to this, which you'll see if you view the browser source of this page:

```
<?
echo "<table>" ;
echo "<tr>" ;
echo "<td><b>Sign:</b></td>" ;
echo "<td><b>Dates:</b></td>" ;
echo "</tr>" ;
echo "<tr>" ;
echo "<td>Libra<td>" ;
echo "<td>23/09-22/10</td>" ;
echo "</tr>" ;
echo "</table>" ;
?>
```

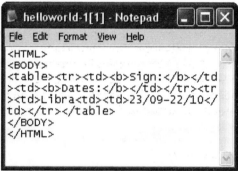

The new lines in the PHP code do not give new lines in the HTML source delivered to the browser. If a page doesn't look right when displayed in the browser, you will want to look at the HTML source as well as the PHP code for debugging purposes – and this will not be easy if the output is all bunched up on one long line. The table created by the source shown above is quite simple, but it is already hard to see where the error is. It would be much easier if we had new lines and tabs spacing the tags out properly.

To insert a new line into the output, you can use the special character \n, and you can insert a tab with \t. But using these and having to escape every dodgy quote character isn't very practical when you have dozens or hundreds of lines of HTML on a page. Fortunately, we don't have to.

Displaying large blocks of text

There are two ways of avoiding the tedious job of formatting the HTML output with new lines, tabs and escape characters. The simplest is to close off one block of PHP code with a ?> tag, and then open a new one next time we need to use some PHP:

```
<?
$sign = "Libra" ;
$dates = "Sept 23 - Oct 22" ;
echo "Here is the horoscope for $sign:" ;
```

The next chunk doesn't contain any PHP, so we just tell the parser to skip it by closing the ?> tag:

```
?>
<table border="1" cellpadding="5" width="100%">
  <tr>
   <td width="80">This week:</td>
   <td>With Mars in the ascendant you'll experi-
ence powerful cravings for chocolate some time
around the 17th, but Mercury's influence (the
"Freddie effect") may restrain your urges -
you'll need to keep the weight off if you want
to look good in Spandex for that big gig!</td>
  </tr>
  <tr>
   <td colspan="2">
```

Now we need to use PHP to handle some variables, so we tell the parser to read the next bit by using more <? ... ?> tags:

```
<? echo "$sign: $dates" ; ?>
```

... and back to plain old HTML again:

```
  </td>
  </tr>
</table>
```

Preserving values

Notice that we defined the variable $dates in one block of PHP, then used it in another block. The value of any variable is preserved between blocks, as long as they are all on the same page. We will look at passing variables between pages in Chapter 5.

The second way of dealing with large blocks of text is to use an echo statement like this:

```
echo <<<END
put your output here on the next line…
… and the next… keep going as long as you like,
just as long as when you're done, you finish off
with END; on a new line.
END;
```

This is useful if the block contains lots of variables, because in this syntax, any variables are evaluated and their value is returned. The <<<END indicates that everything on subsequent lines is to be treated as output, until the parser reaches a new line with END; on it. If END; is not written on a line of its own with the semicolon immediately after it (no space between them), it will just be treated as text output.

In the example above, we had to open a new block of PHP code to get at the values of the variables $sign and $dates. Instead, we could do it like this:

```
<?
$sign = "Libra" ;
$dates = "Sept 23 - Oct 22" ;
echo <<<END
Here is the horoscope for $sign:
<table border="1" cellpadding="5" width="100%">
  <tr>
   <td width="80">This week:</td>
   <td>With Mars in the ascendant you'll experi-
ence powerful cravings for chocolate some time
around the 17th, but Mercury's influence (the
"Freddie effect") may restrain your urges -
you'll need to keep the weight off if you want
to look good in Spandex for that big gig!</td>
  </tr>
  <tr>
   <td colspan="2">$sign: $dates</td>
  </tr>
</table>
END;
?>
```

END and EOF

You may come across variations of this syntax (known as the 'heredoc' syntax) with different start and finish markers. A common one is EOF (End Of File). You can type any marker you like after the <<<, as long as you make sure that you use the same one followed by a semicolon to mark the end.

3.5 Tying and cutting up strings

Concatenation

Since strings are just arbitrarily long sequences of characters, we can take two or more strings and tie them together to create a third, longer string. This is called concatenation, and it is done with the full stop character:

```php
$string1 = "concat" ;
$string2 = "enation" ;
$string3 = $string1 . $string2 ;
echo $string3 ;
```

Which will give us the output concatenation. Notice that no spaces have crept into the third string – the two strings are stuck directly onto each other. If you wanted to build a sentence out of several strings, you would have to make sure you include the spaces – either in the component strings themselves, or separately. Concatenation does not have to work with variables alone; it can include non-variable strings as well:

```php
$string1 = "concatenated strings " ;
$string2 = "are" ;
$string3 = "so much" ;
$string4 = $string1 . $string2 . " " . $string3
. " fun!" ;
echo $string4 ;
```

Output:

concatenated strings are so much fun!

We can do something similar without creating a whole slew of different variables, by taking an initial string and building it up:

```
$string1 = "Beginning," ;
$string1 = $string1 . " middle," ;
$string1 = $string1 . " end." ;
echo $string1 ;
```

Output:

```
Beginning, middle, end.
```

And to save you some typing, PHP supports a shorthand way of doing this: a full stop followed immediately by an equals sign means 'equals whatever it was before plus this new bit'.

```
$string1 = "Beginning," ;
$string1 .= " middle," ;
$string1 .= " end." ;
echo $string1 ;
```

Output:

```
Beginning, middle, end.
```

Substrings

Similarly, we can take a long string and cut it up into smaller substrings if we want to do different things with different parts of it. The most useful PHP function for doing this is substr(), and it takes the following format:

```
substr(string, n, x)
```

Where *string* is the string you start with, *n* is where in the string to start the substring (at the *n*th character of *string*, starting at 0), and *x* is the length (in characters) of the substring.

So to get at the first 3 characters of the string "abcdefghijk" you would do this:

```
$string1 = "abcdefghijk" ;
$string2 = substr($string1, 0, 3) ;
```

To get at the next two characters, you would write:

```
$string2 = substr($string1, 3, 2) ;
```

We will come back to strings in later chapters – there is a huge array of PHP string functions for chopping up and sticking together strings; searching them for substrings, reversing them, exploding them and generally tampering with them in weird and wonderful ways.

3.6 Maths lesson

PHP has all the advanced mathematical functions you'd expect on a swanky scientific calculator – arc tangents and inverse hyperbolic cosines, base-10 and natural logarithms … – as well as random number generators and functions to check whether an expression returns an infinite answer. Great! But for the moment we'll stick to simple arithmetic.

The syntax for basic maths is exactly the same as it was when you learned it at school, only you use the asterisk character to represent multiplication instead of ×, and a forward slash for division instead of ÷.

```php
$result1 = 6 + 3 ; // returns 9
$result2 = 6 - 3 ; // returns 3
$result3 = 6 * 3 ; // returns 18
$result4 = 6 / 3 ; // returns 2
```

Comments in code

All good code is well-documented with plenty of comments to explain what is going on. To add a comment in PHP, use a double forward slash. This tells the parser to ignore anything on the rest of that line, and start scanning again on the next new line.

In more complicated expressions, use brackets to force certain parts to be evaluated before others. Spaces between numbers and symbols are optional: do whatever makes it easiest to read!

```php
$result5 = 6 / (2 * 3) ; // returns 1
```

If you don't make the evaluation order explicit, PHP will perform any division first, then multiplication, then finally addition and subtraction.

```php
$result6 = 6 / 2 * 3 ; // returns 9
$result7 = 6 + (6/3) * ((4+8)/(3*2)) ;
// 1st stage: 6 + 2 * (12/6)
// 2nd stage: 6 + 2 * 2
```

Order of evaluation is no longer explicitly given by brackets; multiplication takes precedence over addition.

```
// 3rd stage: 6 + 4
// returns 10
```

There is a similar shorthand notation for maths as for concatenating strings:

```
$result += 5 ;
// equivalent to $result = $result + 5

$result -= 5 ;
// equivalent to $result = $result - 5

$result *= 5 ;
// equivalent to $result = $result * 5

$result /= 5 ;
// equivalent to $result = $result / 5
```

Maths with variables

Clearly our mathematical functions are going to be most useful when we can apply the same operations to different starting numbers, without having to rewrite a whole chunk of code. For instance, we might have a web page which takes a net invoice amount and calculates the tax:

```
$total = 100 ;
$tax = $total * 17.5 / 100 ;
```

Or to be even more flexible, we could make the tax rate variable. Once we learn how to collect user input via a web form (Chapter 7), we will be able to use a single web page to calculate tax at any rate we like:

```
$total = 100 ;
$taxRate = 9 ;
$tax = $total * $taxRate / 100 ;
```

We can then use our shorthand notation to recalculate the total including tax:

```
$total += $vat ;
```

Remember that the output of a PHP script does not have to be text displayed by the browser: we can use it to write information into HTML tags too. For instance, suppose we want to give the user control over font sizes, to make our page accessible to users with visual impairments. We could create a variable $base which we use in the document's stylesheet to set the normal font size, and then define other font sizes in relation to this one.

```
<? $base = 13 ; ?>
<style type="text/css">
P.normal {font-size: <? echo $base ; ?>px;}
P.small {font-size: <? echo ($base-3) ; ?>px;}
P.large {font-size: <? echo ($base+5) ; ?>px;}
P.huge {font-size: <? echo ($base*3) ; ?>px;}
</style>
```

Now all we have to do is change the value of the $base variable, and all the text of varying sizes across the whole page is updated together. Try changing it yourself and viewing the page:

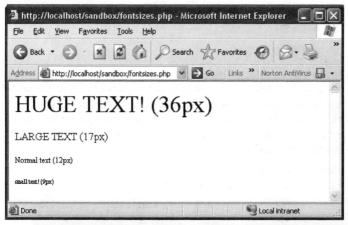

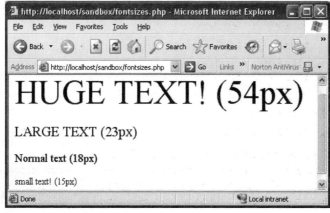

Maths constants

PHP also has a set of predefined mathematical constants, such as pi (`M_PI`) and the square root of two (`M_SQRT2`). You can use these at any time just by dropping them into your calculations. Note that they MUST be uppercase: remember that in PHP names are case-sensitive.

```php
$r = 5 ;
$c = 2 * M_PI * $r ;
$a = M_PI * $r * $r ;
echo "A circle with radius $r has circumference
$c and area $a." ;
```

For a full list of these maths constants, see the PHP manual at www.php.net/manual/en/ref.math.php.

3.7 Arrays

So far we have always assigned a single value to a variable. This one variable, one vote arrangement is called a 'scalar variable'. Variables can also be 'compound', meaning that the relationship is more complex – a compound variable may contain several values. Compound variables include *objects*, which are a little beyond the scope of this book, and *arrays*. An array is a set of variables linked together for some common purpose – for instance, an array `$vital_stats` might contain the elements 'height', 'weight', 'hair_colour' and 'shoe_size'. Each element is actually a pair – a *value* and a *key* which is used to refer to the value. By default, the keys are a numbered index starting at zero, but they can also be named for easier reference.

Defining an array

To define a simple array, use the `array()` function and assign it to a variable name:

```php
$vital_stats = array(185, 155, "black", 42)
```

If we want to give the keys some nice memorable names, use the special operator => like this:

```php
$vital_stats = array("height" => 185, "weight" =>
155, "hair_colour" => "black", "shoe_size" => 42)
```

Using data from an array

This is all very neat, storing related data in a single variable – but how do you get to any particular part of the array without getting the stuff you're not interested in right now? The answer is to use the keys, enclosed in [square brackets] after the variable name.

For instance, `$vital_stats[1]` would refer to the second element in the `$vital_stats` array (remember, the array index starts at zero). In the example above, this would return whatever value had been defined for `weight`. If the array had been defined with named keys, you could get to the same piece of data by using `$vital_stats['weight']`.

Exercises

1 Take the following strings and concatenate them into a single string variable, then display it on-screen.

He said

"Julie baby,

you're my flame"

Remember to escape the three quotes and insert spaces where necessary between words.

2 Given the initial string "You give me fever... fever that's so hard to bear", use `substr()` to isolate the substrings "fever..." and "that's so".

3 Write a script which will take an initial number and perform calculations on it to return the following:

   i)   the number as a percentage of 42

   ii) its square plus half of the original number

   iii) the number minus the square root of two.

Summary

- A variable is a programming concept. It is like the joker in a deck of cards because its face value is not constant.

- Variables can be strings (letters, numbers and other characters) or numbers, and many programming languages have strict rules about what you can do with one type or another.

- PHP is more flexible – it looks at what you are trying to do with a variable and treats it as a string or a number accordingly.

- Strings can be tied together into longer strings or cut up into smaller ones.

- Numbers can be subjected to mathematical functions, using standard notation for arithmetic, as well as more advanced functions.

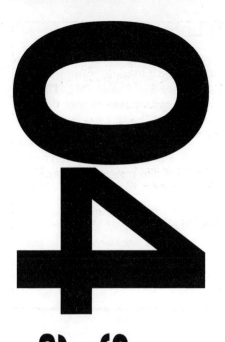

04

statements and loops

In this chapter you will learn:

- about using control structures in PHP

- how to use the if... else... structure

- how to use the while... and do... while... structures

- how to use the for... and foreach... structures

4.1 Control structures

So far, the PHP code we have come across would not be much use in a practical situation. We've used it in static examples which we could have produced much more easily in HTML. The real fun of having a proper programming language at your disposal starts with control structures.

A control structure is a way of getting the PHP parser to look at a variable at a given starting point, and do different things on the basis of what value it has. There are two main circumstances in which you might want to do this.

First, to take some kind of input and return an appropriate output. An example of this might be a script which restricts the user's access to a page depending on the age they claim to be:

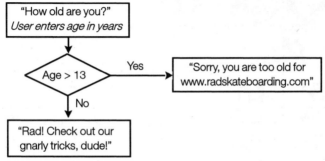

The second kind of control structure is used for *iterative* functions – processes which are repeated many times, but which we only want to code once. To write a counting script which outputs the numbers one to a hundred, we could do something like this:

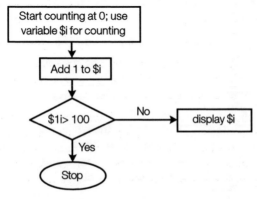

The code needed to do this would only run to a few lines – far fewer than if you tried to code it all up in static HTML. Instead of writing out a hundred separate instructions, the code just loops through the central section as many times as necessary. Then, when a certain condition is fulfilled (in this case, when $i is greater than 100), the code breaks out of the loop and carries on with the next set of instructions.

Comparison operators

To build any kind of control structure, you need a *truth condition* – a statement which can be tested to give the answer 'true' or 'false'. You are probably familiar with the common comparison operators > (greater than) and < (less than). There are also some more subtle operators which you will need to know about if you want to build effective structures.

$a < $b	Less than	TRUE if $a is less than $b.
$a > $b	Greater than	TRUE if $a is greater than $b.
$a <= $b	Less than or equal to	TRUE if $a is less than or equal to $b.
$a >= $b	Greater than or equal to	TRUE if $a is greater than or equal to $b.
$a == $b	Equal	TRUE if $a is equal to $b.
$a != $b	Not equal	TRUE if $a is not equal to $b.
$a === $b	Identical	TRUE if $a is equal to $b, and they are of the same type.
$a !== $b	Not identical	TRUE if $a is not equal to $b, or they are not of the same type.

The first four operators are straightforward enough, but take a good look at the various different kinds of 'equals' we have. Notice that there is no single equals sign in the table above.

The normal way of asking whether something equals something else is to use the double equals sign (==). The triple equals sign not only compares the two values, but also the value types. Although the PHP parser will treat a string as a number if it can (and vice versa), it still knows what kind of value it originally was. In practice you will probably not use this very often, but it's nice to know you can.

For example, suppose we define $a as the number 10:

```
$a = 10
```

Single '=' assigns value.

```
($a == 10)
```

Double '==' tests that values are equal. This returns TRUE.

```
($a == "10")
```

This also returns TRUE.

```
($a === 10)
```

Triple '===' tests that values are identical. This returns TRUE.

```
($a === "10")
```

But this returns FALSE, since $a is a number but "10" is a string.

4.2 If... Else...

This is the classic programming structure – if a certain condition is met, do X; if not, do Y. In PHP the syntax is as follows:

```
if (condition) {
   do this ;
} else {
   do that ;
}
```

The condition to be tested is set out in normal (rounded brackets), and the actions to be taken are enclosed in {curly braces}. These don't have to go onto new lines, but the convention is to do this, and to indent them – it just makes it easier to read.

If we apply this to our skateboarder's example above, we could end up with something like this:

```
<?
$age = 12 ;
if ($age > 13) {
   echo "Sorry, you can't come in." ;
} else {
```

```
   echo "Welcome! <A HREF='home.php'>Click here
to enter</A>" ;
}
?>
```

Try this script with different starting values for $age and check the results in your browser.

The ternary operator

This is a compact alternative to the if... else... structure, used when the two alternatives on offer are little bite-sized pieces of code rather than long blocks of code. It looks like this:

```
(condition) ? expression1 : expression2
```

If the condition evaluates to TRUE, then expression1 is returned, otherwise expression2 is returned. Since the ternary operator returns a value, it is used inside another expression, such as one assigning a value to a variable. In the following example, the ternary operator looks at a variable called $time, and returns "afternoon" if it is 12 o'clock or later, or "morning" otherwise:

```
$am_or_pm = ($time>=12) ? "afternoon" : "morning" ;
echo "Good $am_or_pm!" ;
```

If... Elseif... Else...

We can expand the if... else... structure to include more complex situations than a simple either/or scenario. To do this, we insert an elseif for each new condition after the first if:

```
if (first condition) {
   do this ;
} elseif (second condition) {
   do that ;
} else {
   do the other ;
}
```

You could repeat this any number of times, with a new elseif... for each new condition. There should always be an else... at the end of the structure as a catch-all device – just in case the actual course of events doesn't meet any of the specific conditions you set out.

For instance the example above could be added to like this:

```
<?
$age = 2 ;
if ($age > 13) {
    echo "Sorry, you can't come in." ;
} elseif ($age <= 3) {
    echo "Ooh you liar! Get out." ;
} else {
    echo "Welcome! <A HREF='home.php'>Click here
to enter</A>" ;
}
?>
```

Just if...

We can also use a simpler form of the structure, which has no else..., just an if.... This is useful when you want to perform some action if a condition is true, but not do anything at all if it isn't. For instance, here's an if... which adds a plural "s" onto a word if the number is plural, but leaves it alone if not:

```
<?
$age = 30 ;
echo "You are $age year" ;
if ($age > 1) {
    echo "s" ;
}
echo " old" ;
?>
```

Try it with different values for $age.

Iffy ifs

Be careful when building control structures with several 'if' conditions – you should try to ensure that the result cannot match more than one condition. When the PHP parser goes through an if... elseif... else... structure, it will stop as soon as it finds a good match. Suppose you had:

```
if ($age > 10) {
    echo "11-16 years old." ;
} elseif ($age > 16) {
```

```
      echo "Over 16." ;
   } else {
      echo "Ten or under." ;
   }
```

This would give the right result if $age was 11 or 14, but if you tried it with $age as 20, you would still get the first message – the first TRUE condition which the parser encounters – but it is now wrong. To avoid this, you can list your conditions in such a way that the first TRUE condition gives you the answer you need.

```
   if ($age > 16) {
      echo "Over 16." ;
   } elseif ($age > 10) {
      echo "11-16 years old." ;
   } else {
      echo "Ten or under." ;
   }
```

Clearly this could be a real headache, so it is better to make the conditions tighter and mutually exclusive instead.

Complex conditions

What if the condition we want to test for involves more than one factor? Suppose you want to look at two or three variables and provide different outcomes depending on their combination. There are two ways to approach this: the first is to set out a combination of conditions; if they all evaluate to TRUE, then perform some action. Each individual condition to test for is enclosed in brackets, and they are joined by a double ampersand (&&) and the whole lot enclosed in another set of brackets.

```
   if ( ($col == "grey") && ($size == "big") ) {
      echo "That's probably an elephant." ;
   } else {
      echo "No, that can't be an elephant." ;
   }
```

Alternatively, you could check to see if either one or another of two different conditions is met. This uses the OR operator (||) instead of the AND (&&).

```
   if ( ($size == "big") || ($size == "huge") ) {
      echo "Well it's big enough to be an elephant." ;
```

```
    } else {
        echo "Sorry, that's too small for an elephant." ;
    }
```

We can build up the complexity by including new conditions to be met and combining them with the AND operator (&&) or the OR operator (||), adding brackets as necessary to clarify what the OR applies to.

```
    if ( ($col == "grey") && ( ($size == "big") ||
    ($size == "huge") ) && ($trunk == TRUE) ) {
        echo "Yep, that's definitely an elephant." ;
    } else {
        echo "Sorry, no way is that an elephant." ;
    }
```

Readable code

When there are several conditions combined like this, it can get hard to read. If so, you can just break them up over several lines to clarify what's going on:

```
    if (($col == "grey") &&
        (($size == "big") || ($size == "huge")) &&
        ($trunk == TRUE)) {
```

Nested structures

An alternative approach, which can be more appropriate when you're dealing with a large number of possible combinations, is to *nest* a series of if... else... structures to build a branching structure. This can give you fine control over your conditions without having to repeat yourself. The next example will examine three animal characteristics and try to determine a mystery animal, depending on how they combine.

When you have several conditions acting in combination, it's a good idea to sketch out the branching on paper first, before getting tangled up in brackets, braces and ampersands. You may find that you can reduce the complexity by testing the conditions in different orders – and you'll certainly get it straighter in your head before you start coding, which always helps!

Start by listing the variables and their possible values.

```
$size // can be "big" or "small"
$col // can be anything, but we're looking for
"grey"
$hasFur // can be TRUE or FALSE
```

True or false?

Note that we are defining $hasFur as a Boolean variable, which takes the value TRUE or FALSE. When we assign a value to it, we do not use quotes (that would signal that it is a string, not a Boolean):

```
$hasFur = TRUE ;
```

This can also be written with the shorthand 1 for TRUE and 0 for FALSE:

```
$hasFur = 1 ;
```

Now list the possible outcomes, and what combination of variables is needed to produce them.

```
Elephant - big, grey, no fur
Mouse - small, grey, furry
woodlouse - small, grey, no fur
```

This will help you realize if the variables are going to give you enough information to determine the outcome accurately. For instance, if we included sea creatures in our animal-identifier, we would not be able to distinguish whales (big, grey, no fur) from elephants, and would need to check for a fourth condition such as $hasFins.

Now sketch out a flowchart to illustrate the process of narrowing down the combination of variables to produce the right outcome. The goal should be to get to the answer as quickly as possible, without asking unnecessary questions, or asking the same question more times than we have to.

So in this example, we would start by asking 'Is the mystery animal grey?' – if it's not grey, there's no point asking any of the other questions because our animal-identifier only knows grey animals. If we asked 'Is it big?' to start with, then regardless of the answer we would still have to ask whether it is grey, which means we would have to nest the 'Is it grey?' condition twice.

If you start by testing the broadest conditions first and then refine your criteria with each nested condition, you should end up with the simplest solution possible. This will make life a lot easier when trying to track down faulty logic!

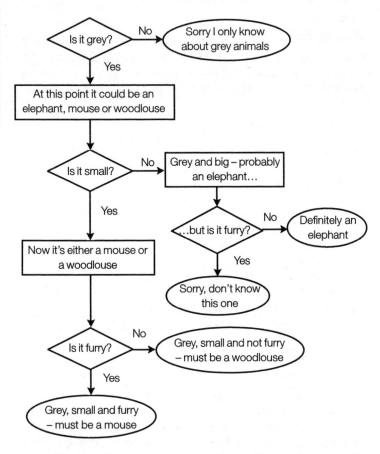

Now we are in a position to start writing some code. When building up a set of nested structures like this, it can get confusing if you try to write it out in one go, first line to last – all you have to do is miss one curly brace out and everything goes wonky. I usually start by writing out the outermost structure in full, leaving a space (and sometimes a note-to-self) for the next layer of nesting. Then I go back and repeat the process for the next layer, and so on. So after the first pass, it would look like this:

```
if ($col == "grey") {
   // other ifs go here…
} else {
   $msg = "Sorry, I only know grey animals." ;
}
echo $msg ;
```

If you are feeling thorough, you could test the script out with
different values of $col at this point, just to make sure there are
no errors so far. Assuming it is working well, move on to the next
layer, and then the next, testing between each layer to check for
errors.

```
if ($col == "grey") {
   // at this point it's any grey animal
   if ($size == "small") {
      // now it's either a mouse or a woodlouse
      if ($hasFur == TRUE) {
         $msg = "Eeek! A mouse!" ;
      } else {
         $msg = "It's a woodlouse." ;
      }
   } else {
// this "else" refers to $size, i.e. not small
// we know it's big and grey – what about fur?
      if ($hasFur == TRUE) {
         $msg = "Um… Is it a radioactive mouse?" ;
      } else {
         $msg = "That'll be an elephant then." ;
      }
   }
// the brace above ends the $size if… else…
} else {
   // this "else" refers to $col, i.e. not grey
   $msg = "Sorry, I only know grey animals." ;
}
echo $msg ;
```

Try this out in your browser, assigning different values to $col,
$size, and $hasFur. If you like, add extra echo statements to
show which values lead to the outcome shown in the screenshot
on the next page.

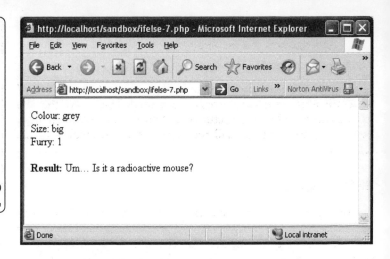

Debugging control structures

If a nested structure is giving you unwanted results, you should comment out all but the outermost structure, and test the script using two variables which should produce a TRUE and a FALSE for that condition. If that part of the structure is behaving as it should, un-comment the next layer of nesting and test that. If you need to, add temporary echo statements so that you can see clearly what stage of the branching structure you reach each time.

4.3 While... and Do... While...

The while... and do... while... structures are useful for looping through an instruction or set of instructions which you want the script to carry out several times before moving on. They basically say 'as long as condition X is true, keep doing action A', and the syntax is as follows.

```
while (condition) {

    statements to be executed ;

}
```

And:

```
do {
    statements to be executed ;
} while (condition) ;
```

The only difference between them is when the condition is checked
– before or after the statements are executed. This means that the
statements in a while... structure might not even be executed once,
whereas a do... while... will run at least once, regardless of the
condition.

Infinite loops

Normally, one of the statements inside the loop must have some
effect on the conditional variable – because if the condition never
changes, then the parser can get stuck in the loop. It will perform
the same actions over and over again until somebody (or some
server maintenance routine) notices what has happened and shuts
the process down.

At some point, something like this is almost bound to happen to
you, so you might as well do it once deliberately so that you
recognize it when it does happen, and you know how to deal
with it. Try viewing a page with this code in a browser...

```
$i = 0 ;
while ($i < 1) {
    echo "DOH! " ;
}
```

When it gets stuck, you can try stopping the page loading, but to
no avail. You will probably need to stop the server (use the Apache
icon in the system tray). You may also need to press
[Ctrl]+[Alt]+[Delete] and shut down your browser if it has
stopped responding. Remember to start the server again once
you've sorted out the browser!

Useful loops

It follows from the section above that the only useful kind of loop
(unless you're deliberately trying to crash people's machines) is a
finite loop. To build a good loop we need a definite beginning
and end. In this example, we want to write something 100 times,
so we create a variable $i and assign it the initial value of 1.

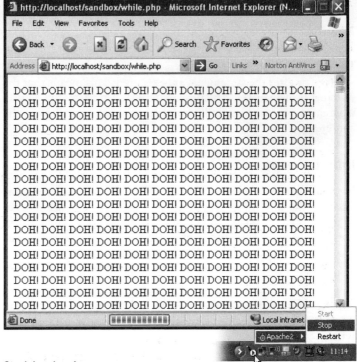

Stuck in a loop!

Then we set up a while… loop to print out our message. If we increase $i by one every time we go through the loop, $i will eventually reach a hundred, and we can tell the parser to stop going through the loop.

```php
$i = 1 ;
while ($i <= 100) {
    echo "I must not use PHP to write my punish-
ment lines." ;
    $i++ ;
}
```

Notice the use of $i++ here. This means $i = $i+1, which is used so often that it gets its own special shorthand. Similarly, you can decrement a number by using $i--.

4.4 For...

The for... structure is similar to do... while.... It is also used to build loops, but is a slightly quicker, more compact way of doing so. The syntax looks like this:

```
for (start; condition; loop;) {
    statements ;
}
```

start is an expression which is executed once only, at the beginning of the loop;

condition is the truth condition, which is tested *before* each pass through the loop;

loop is an expression executed at the end of each loop (i.e. the expression which feeds back into the truth condition to stop the loop going on for ever);

statements are the other statements executed on each pass through the loop.

The while... example above could be written using for... instead, with $i=1 as the **start** expression and $i++ as the **loop**.

```
for ($i=1; $i<=100; $i++;) {
    echo "I must not use PHP to write my punish-
ment lines." ;
}
```

4.5 Foreach...

The foreach... structure is specifically for use with arrays. It is used to go through an array performing the same process on each element in turn. There are two slightly different forms of the syntax for it:

```
foreach ($array as $value;) {
    statements using $value ;
}
```

and:

```
foreach ($array as $key => $value;) {
    statements using $key and $value ;
}
```

So for instance we might use the first like this:

```
$team = array("Jean", "Bob", "Parvez", "Alice") ;
echo "The line-up this week is:<P>" ;
foreach ($team as $player) {
    echo "$player<BR/>" ;
}
```

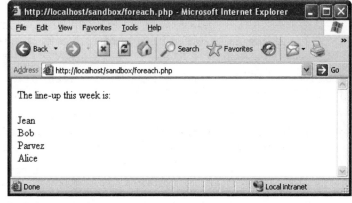

And the second one could give us a bit more information:

```
$team = array("Jean" => "left wing", "Bob" =>
"defence", "Parvez" => "midfield", "Alice" =>
"right wing") ;
echo "The line-up this week is:<P>" ;
foreach ($team as $player => $position) {
    echo "$player ($position)<BR/>" ;
}
```

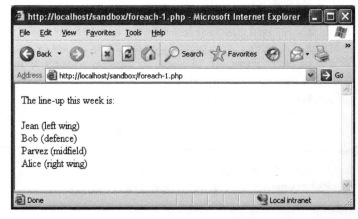

Exercises

1 Write a script with a variable called $lang, whic[h ... giv]es a different welcome message depending on the valu[e given] to $lang.

   Hint: if you only speak one language, try Google's t[ranslator] (follow the Language Tools link)!

2 You love garlic and quite like beans, but you hate anything containing parsnips: write a script to assess how much you might like a certain meal, depending on which of these ingredients it contains.

3 Write a script with a loop to output the lyrics to '99 bottles of beer on the wall'.

4 If you haven't already, now add some variables and an if... structure into the script to ensure that when you get down to a single beer, the word 'bottle' is not plural.

   Hint: watch out for the last line – 0 bottles needs to be plural again.

Summary

- Control structures are used to produce outputs which vary according to the script's inputs.

- There are two main types: if... else... structures and loops (while..., do... while... and for...).

- All control structures need a truth condition to evaluate, the result of which determines what action is taken next.

- Any loop should have an expression in it which affects the truth condition variable, in order to avoid infinite looping.

05

talking to the browser

In this chapter you will learn:

- about predefined variables
- how to get information about the browser
- how to pass information to a page using the URL
- how to create real (almost) dynamic pages

5.1 Predefined variables

So far, our experience of variables has been one of god-like power – you can create a variable and call it whatever you like (within a few minor rules) and assign any value you fancy to it. But there are also a number of predefined variables which are used to get at information beyond the confines of your script. These are created at the server, using predefined names – which you need to know if you are going to make use of them. For instance, there are predefined variables which refer to properties of the server delivering your pages, or the browser through which the user is viewing your page.

Why might you want to know this? There are several possible reasons. If you've ever built a web page and had to compromise to make it work in different browsers, you might have wished you could just design separate pages for each browser. This is especially true if your pages use a lot of client-side code – you have probably used Javascript 'browser sniffers' to work out what the user has, but it may be more efficient to let the server work out which browser is being used and send only the code it needs.

You might want to know whether your site's getting a lot of international traffic, and perhaps greet visitors in their own language. You might want to know how the visitor found your site – trace the link back from your page to the 'referrer' to find out who's been linking to your site.

Or ... you might just be nosey. Here's how you do it, anyway.

5.2 Getting information about the browser

Try viewing a page with this code in your browser:

```
<?
$browser = $_SERVER['HTTP_USER_AGENT'] ;
echo "The sniffer says: $browser" ;
?>
```

You should get a result something like the following screenshot.

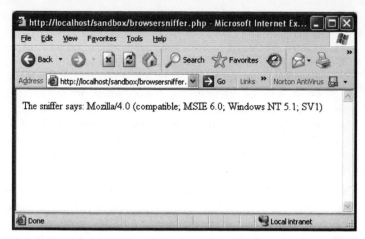

The name of the variable you want to access is HTTP_USER_AGENT, and you have to request it from an array of predefined variables called $_SERVER. The general syntax is:

```
$_SERVER['VARIABLE']
```

... where VARIABLE is replaced by the name of the variable you want. Here are some other variable names you may find useful:

PHP_SELF	The path to the current script.
SERVER_NAME	The server your script is running on.
HTTP_USER_AGENT	The user's browser and operating system details.
HTTP_REFERER	If the user arrived at this page by following a link from another page, this gives the URL of that page.
HTTP_ACCEPT_LANGUAGE	Language settings on the user's browser, in code form – e.g. en-gb for UK English, fr for French, es-mx for Mexican Spanish.

Using browser information to customize display

Let's combine a request with an If... Else... structure to tailor our page to an international audience:

```
<?
$lang = $_SERVER['HTTP_ACCEPT_LANGUAGE'] ;
```

```
if ($lang == "en-gb") {
    echo "HELLO! Would you like a cup of tea?" ;
} elseif ($lang == "fr") {
    echo "BONJOUR! Voulez-vous un croissant?" ;
} elseif ($lang="es-mx") {
    echo "HOLA! Quieres un taco al pastor?" ;
} else {
    echo "Hi. Not sure where you're from, but
welcome anyway!" ;
}
?>
```

If you're in the UK, you probably get the first message when you run this script, though if your browser settings include other languages, or US English, you might see the last one instead.

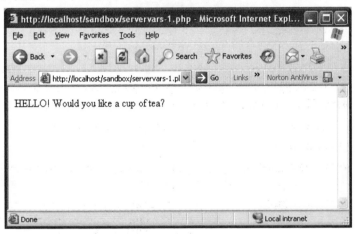

To test the script properly, you'll need to adjust the language settings on your browser (we could write a script to deal with multiple language settings, but it would need some tools we won't come across until Chapter 7).

If you use Internet Explorer:

Select **Tools** on the browser's menu bar, choose **Internet Options** and then click the **Languages...** button.

If you use Netscape Navigator:

Select **Edit** on the browser's menu bar, choose **Preferences** and then select the **Navigator – Languages** category.

You will see a dialog box with a list of languages. Select them one by one and click **Remove** until they are all gone (don't worry, you can put them back in later!).

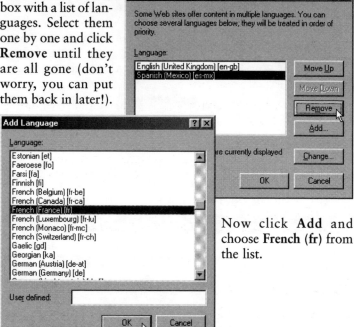

Now click **Add** and choose **French (fr)** from the list.

Close the dialog boxes and reload the page.

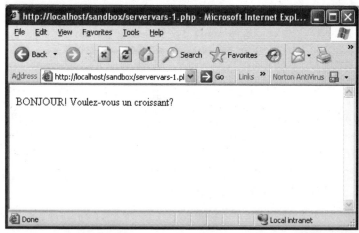

Remember to reset your language when you've finished messing around!

5.3 Passing information using the URL

You have probably noticed web pages with long addresses, punctuated with lots of &s and =s and ?s. These are called query strings and they pass information from one page to another using the URL. Each piece of information is a variable with a name and a value, so for instance you might see the URL:

```
http://www.typhp.com/preview.php?chapter=5&page
=85&mode=free
```

The question mark after the filename indicates that there are variables to follow, and each name–value pair is joined by an equals sign. Where there is more than one variable, the pairs are separated by an ampersand.

So the URL above tells the server to send the page `preview.php` to the browser, along with the following information:

```
chapter = 5

page = 85

mode = free
```

Query strings may be added to a URL using a form which handles lots of information, but you can also add them onto an ordinary link by simply typing them into the HREF tag:

```
<A HREF="preview.php?chapter=5&mode=free"> Pre-
view Chapter Five for free!</a>
```

Getting information from the query string

The information is there in the URL, but our PHP script cannot use it yet. If we just try to echo `$chapter` to a page, nothing will happen – even if there is a `chapter=xxx` given in the URL. This is because as far as the page is concerned, the name–value pairs in the query string are not yet variables in their own right – they are part of an array called `$_GET`. We can either refer to them using the same syntax for the `$_SERVER` variables:

```
$_GET['$chapter']
```

Or if you plan to use the variable more than once, it's probably worth assigning it to a variable that the script will recognize properly:

```
$chap = $_GET['$chapter'] ;
```

NOTE: You don't have to give the variables in the script the same name as the variables passed in the URL. Some people prefer to use different names to distinguish them, I find it less confusing to use the same names ... it's up to you!

$_GET and other superglobals

You may have suspected that the $_GET array has something to do with the GET method of sending information via an HTML form, and you are right. Form data sent via GET is passed into the query string, which in PHP is stored in the $_GET array. Similar arrays exist for form data sent via the POST method ($_POST), and for data stored in cookies ($_COOKIES).

We will look at both of these in detail later in the book, but it may be useful to note now that the contents of $_GET, $_POST, and $_COOKIES are also collected into one associative array called $_REQUEST.

Predefined variables like these are called 'superglobals' because they are automatically available to any part of a PHP script, even inside functions (see the next chapter for more on this).

Using information from the query string

Once the information has been requested and stored in local variables, we can use it wherever we need it. Type up the script below and save it as *passurl.php*.

```
<?
$chap = $_GET['chapter'] ;
$mode = $_GET['mode'] ;
echo "You are about to preview Chapter $chap in
$mode mode. Hope you enjoy it!" ;
?>
```

Now view the page in a browser – remember to type the full URL including the query string into the address bar:

```
passurl.php?chapter=5&mode=free
```

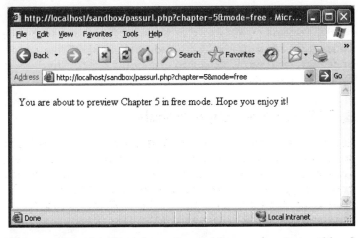

Now try changing the values given in the query string and loading the page again:

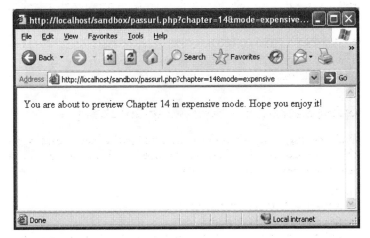

5.4 Your first (almost) dynamic page

In this example we'll use variables to determine the text and background colour attributes of the HTML <BODY> tag. If the variable is requested from the query string, then whatever value is given in the URL will be slotted into the <BODY> tag, and the background colour will change accordingly.

Add the following lines to the <HEAD> section of a page:

```
<?
$bgCol = $_GET['bg'] ;
$txCol = $_GET['tx'] ;
?>
```

Then continue in HTML, inserting the values into the <BODY> tag:

```
<BODY BGCOLOR="<% echo $bgCol %>" TEXT="<% echo
$txCol %>">
```

Now take a look in the browser, using a URL with a query string which includes some recognized HTML colours:

```
colours.php?bg=blue&tx=white
```

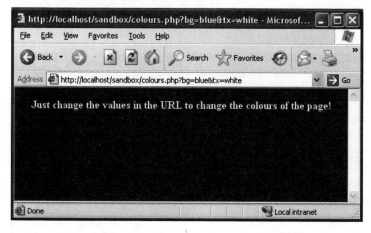

You can also use hex values to specify the colour, but be sure to omit the hash symbol – in a URL, this indicates a bookmark or anchor tag somewhere in the page.

Error-trapping

Before we go any further, try viewing the page above, but without any information in the query string – just enter the URL colours.php into the address bar. Depending on the error reporting settings in your PHP config file, you will probably get some error messages like this:

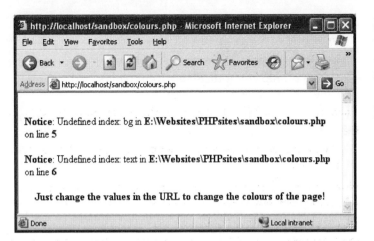

They are not critical errors, because you can see that the rest of the page has been displayed, using the default black text and white background. On most production servers, the error reporting level is turned down so that non-critical errors are hidden. However, it's good practice to write code which is robust enough to survive a little human stupidity, so we should add in a check to trap possible errors. It should find out whether the right data has been passed via the URL, and set default values if it hasn't.

Luckily – as so often with PHP – there is a perfect function for performing this kind of check, called `array_key_exists()`. It takes two arguments, the name of the thing we are checking for, and the array itself. To error-proof the code above, do this:

```
<?
if (array_key_exists('bg', $_GET)) {
    $bgCol = $_GET['bg'] ;
} else {
    $bgCol = "#FFFFFF" ;
}
```

Or for a neater, more compact solution, we could use the ternary operator:

```
$txCol = array_key_exists('tx', $_GET) ?
$_GET['tx'] : "#000000" ;
?>
```

A bit more dynamism

So far, so good – but it's not very impressive to have to type things into the URL, is it? What we really want is a form, where the user is prompted for their favourite colours, and a button to reload the page using those colours.

Unfortunately, you'll have to read the next chapter to start working with forms (sorry), but all is not lost – we can go halfway with what we already know. Instead of a fully user-oriented page with form fields, we can do the next best thing and provide a series of links which can be clicked to change the colours.

Let's start with the background colour. We'll insert a few links, each one pointing to the same page (the current page), but giving different information in the query string. Add the following code to your page, then reload it and try the links.

```
<P>BACKGROUND:
<A HREF="colours.php?bg=FF0000">red</A> ~
<A HREF="colours.php?bg=00FF00">green</A> ~
<A HREF="colours.php?bg=0000FF">blue</A> ~
<A HREF="colours.php?bg=FFFFFF">white</A>
```

Now add some similar code to control the text colour:

```
<P>TEXT:
<A HREF="colours.php?tx=FF0000">red</A> ~
<A HREF="colours.php?tx=00FF00">green</A> ~
<A HREF="colours.php?tx=0000FF">blue</A> ~
<A HREF="colours.php?tx=FFFFFF">white</A>
```

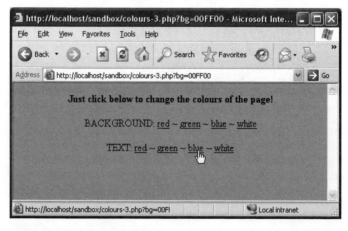

Keeping one variable while changing another

You'll notice that when you click on the links in this example, you lose one colour variable every time you change another. You have a nice green background, but when you click on a link to turn the text red, the background defaults to white.

This is because you're only passing one variable into the URL via the link. The other one is not given there, so it uses the default value instead. But we do have that information to hand – we're already using it in the <BODY> tag – so there's no reason why we shouldn't insert it into a text-changing link as well:

```
<A HREF="colours.php?bg=<? echo $bgCol
?>&tx=FF0000">red</a>
```

Now whenever you change the background colour, you are also dynamically changing the link. Try changing just this one link, then reload the page and change the background colour. Look at the source code to check that the variable is being picked up and used correctly.

Now do the same with the $textCol variable in the background-changing links: you should end up with a revised section of code which looks like this:

```
<P>BACKGROUND:
<A HREF="colours.php?bg=FF0000&tx=<? echo $txCol
?>">red</A> ~
<A HREF="colours.php?bg=00FF00&tx=<? echo $txCol
?>">green</A> ~
<A HREF="colours.php?bg=0000FF&tx=<? echo $txCol
?>">blue</A> ~
<A HREF="colours.php?bg=FFFFFF&tx=<? echo $txCol
?>">white</A>

<P>TEXT:
<A HREF="colours.php?bg=<? echo $bgCol
?>&tx=FF0000">red</A> ~
<A HREF="colours.php?bg=<? echo $bgCol
?>&tx=00FF00">green</A> ~
<A HREF="colours.php?bg=<? echo $bgCol
?>&tx=0000FF">blue</A> ~
<A HREF="colours.php?bg=<? echo $bgCol
?>&tx=FFFFFF">white</A>
```

Save and reload the page – now you should find that the background and text colours can be changed without affecting each other.

You now have what could reasonably be called a dynamic page – 16 different pages, in fact, in about 20 lines of code! In the next chapter we'll look at using forms to collect information from the user and then use it to create really dynamic pages.

Exercises

1   Use the predefined $_SERVER variables to construct a page with two links on it: one to reload the same page, and one to take the user back to the referring page (you will need to write a 'launch' page linking to this page so that there is a referrer to go back to).

2   If you have not already, add some error-trapping in to prevent an error message if there is no referring page to go back to.

3   Write a few simple stylesheets which will give very different appearances when applied to a page, then build a page which uses the query string to apply them to itself. Remember to provide a default stylesheet in case none is specified in the URL.

Summary

- As well as creating your own variables, you can use PHP's predefined variables.

- These give you access to extra information about the server, the user's browser, etc.

- Predefined variables are stored in arrays called superglobals, such as $_SERVER.

- Other superglobals contain data sent to the page via a form or the page's URL ($_GET and $_POST).

- A variable stored in a superglobal can be accessed like any other array: $_ARRAY['variable'].

- Variables can be passed from one page to another (or from one page to a new version of itself) by adding it to the URL referenced in an <A HREF...> tag.

06

PHP for efficient HTML

In this chapter you will learn:

- how to use PHP to write more efficient HTML pages
- how to include modules of code in multiple pages
- how to write functions to carry out processing tasks
- about variable scope

6.1 PHP for more efficient pages

If you have ever maintained a static HTML site, you will know how annoying it is to update elements which are common to all pages. A change to the navigation bar or the top banner, for instance, needs to be implemented across *every single* page on the site (unless of course you were still using frames, which you shouldn't be!). Copy, paste, check ... copy, paste, check – oops, pasted over an extra line and now the page looks horrible – go back and re-paste, check ... copy, paste, check ... what a dull job.

Wouldn't it be nice if you could write these repeated sections just once and reuse them wherever necessary? Then when you need to update something, you only have to do it once, and the change is immediately implemented across all relevant pages. Good news: that's exactly what the `include()` function does in PHP.

Functions

The vast array of functions provided in PHP mean that there is often a piece of code which will do exactly what you need. But

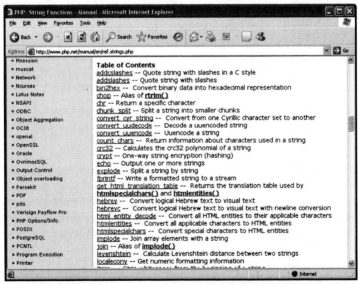

This screenshot shows fewer than half of PHP's predefined string functions – that's just the functions used for manipulating strings. And there are 144 other collections of functions besides string-related ones!

any website is going to have its own peculiar requirements, and you will need to combine PHP's predefined functions to build the code you need to meet them. But imagine how handy it would be if you could take a block of code like this and define it as your own function. Next time you need to perform the same process, you can just call up the function, feed it fresh input variables – and as my old maths teacher used to say, 'Robert is the brother of your parent'.

6.2 Using included files

Better than frames

In the bad old days, HTML coders used to use framesets and frames to build pages with common elements such as banners or navigation panels. Then we realized that this caused headaches with search engines – either you banned search bots from indexing anything beneath your frameset page (not much use), or you risk people arriving at a page without a frameset, so they have no way of getting to the rest of your site. There are ways around it, but they're messy – and more important, there are serious accessibility issues with framesets. Users who are restricted to keyboard control for any reason have no way of getting from one frame to another, so they simply cannot access most of your content. Very bad – not to mention illegal (in the UK at least) since the DDA (Disability Discrimination Act) came into force.

Fortunately, languages like PHP have come to our rescue with the concept of included files, also known as 'server side includes' or SSIs. An included file is a code module saved as a file which can be called from any given page, and its contents included in that page before it is sent to the browser. It may be a tiny snippet of code, or a lengthy and complicated script; it may be pure HTML, pure PHP or a mixture of both. The important thing to note is that included files are drawn into the main body of the page *before* any scripting in them is processed. This means that they can use variables defined in the main page, and vice versa.

Other uses of included files

The uses of included files extend way beyond merely replacing framesets. An included file might contain HTML which you want to use in various places for the same chunk of display material – a price list for instance, or some linked images. It might contain just a tiny fragment of text – suppose you are a widget manufacturer, and your website features a Widget of the Week, which is referred to on numerous pages. The included file could just be the name of this week's widget, or the name plus a link to more information.

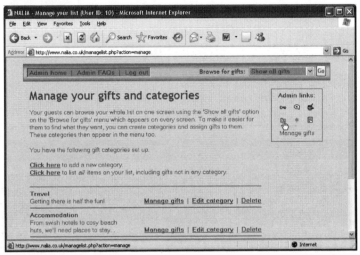

The 'quick links' box at the top right is an included file, used on all the admin pages of this site.

An included file does not have to produce anything visible in the browser at all – it could contain some PHP functions you have defined and are likely to need in several places. Or perhaps a set of client-side scripts which you often want to use on your pages – pop-up window code, for instance, or some DHTML effects. It could contain a simple list of variables used by a page (or pages), which can be used for routine content updates, even by someone with no web skills at all. Suppose you have a page with a diagram of a football field and the various positions marked out with the players' names for the next match – all neatly coded, and you'd be understandably reluctant to let the office temp anywhere near it. But if you use variables for the names and assign their values in a short included file, you could safely train pretty much anyone to edit and upload it.

Creating and calling an included file

Enough theory – let's create and use some included files. A very simple included file might just contain this simple piece of text:

```
Moses
```

Save the file somewhere in your web directory as `myname.php`. It could also be called `myname.txt` or `myname.htm` – PHP is not fussy (I generally stick to the `.txt` or `.php` extensions, mainly so I don't confuse myself). Now, to include the file in another php file, you need to call it using the `include()` function:

```
<?
echo "Hello, my name is " ;
include 'includes/myname.php' ;
echo ". Nice to meet you." ;
?>
```

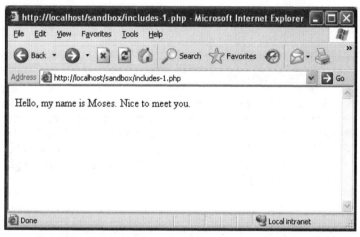

The file to be included – including its path relative to the file which is calling it – is enclosed in single quotes. The PHP parser goes off to the specified location, reads the file and drops its contents into place.

That seems straightforward enough, but if you look carefully, something does not seem quite right. If we were to go and do the parser's job ourselves – as described above – we might expect to end up with something like this:

```
<?
echo "Hello, my name is " ;
```

```
Moses
echo ". Nice to meet you." ;
?>
```

Clearly, this won't work, because the parser is going to try to execute Moses as if it were a PHP statement of some kind. In fact, what happens is slightly counter-intuitive. When reading an included file, the PHP parser drops out of PHP mode and back into HTML mode. Effectively, when it pulls the contents of the included file into the main file, it closes off the previous block of PHP code, dumps the contents in, and then opens a new block to continue:

```
<?
echo "Hello, my name is " ;
?>
Moses
<?
echo ". Nice to meet you." ;
?>
```

PHP in included files

If an included file is to contain any PHP code which we want to be executed, we need to enclose it in <? ?> PHP tags – even if the whole lot is PHP, we still need to start it all with a <? and end it with a ?>. For instance, suppose we want to use an included file to give easy access to a couple of variables. The main page might contain code like this:

```
<?
include 'includes/scores.php' ;
echo "Today's high scorer is $hiscore... " ;
echo "...and today's loser is $loscore!" ;
?>
```

Then our included file could look like this:

```
<?
$hiscore = "Sybilla" ;
$loscore = "Suzie" ;
?>
```

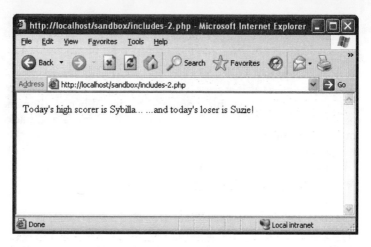

Let's try a situation in which variables are passed in both directions – i.e. from the main file to the included file, and from the included to the main file. Imagine we have a site with some common information which is the same across the whole site – site name, for instance, and a contact e-mail address. Then we have some information which varies from page to page, such as the page title and the background colour. To put this together, we might first write out one page in plain HTML. Looking at this, we can see what will be common to other similar pages – and can therefore be stashed in included pages – and what will need to stay page-specific.

```
<HTML>
<HEAD>
<TITLE>The Autumn Collection</TITLE>
</HEAD>
<BODY BGCOLOR="#D0B283">
<H2>AnorakWorld: The Autumn Collection</H2>
Our seasonal speciality is the brown cagoule.
<BR/> <BR/>
For more info, email <A
HREF="mailto:me@akw.com">me@akw.com</a>.
</BODY>
</HTML>
```

All pages on the AnorakWorld site are going to start with the <HTML> and <HEAD> tags, so these can certainly go into a included file called *header.php* (we should also really put in some standard metadata like the DOCTYPE and CHARSET, but I don't want to clutter up the page with unhelpful code at this point). All pages will also have <TITLE> and <BODY> tags, but their content may vary – the Spring Collection page might have a green background instead of brown. We can either leave this section in every individual page, or we can put it into *header.php* along with some variables which will be picked up from each page:

```
header.php

<HTML>
<HEAD>
<TITLE><? echo $page ; ?></TITLE>
</HEAD>
<BODY BGCOLOR="<? echo $bg ; ?>">
```

The next section of code deals with the displayed title and text. This includes the site name and some page-specific content which may or may not include the site administrator's e-mail address. Most of this content is going to vary from one page to the next, so it is not suitable for including. We might want to make the site name and e-mail address into variables, just in case they change (you know what the marketing department can be like …). This means we need to go back to *header.php* and define these variables there. We also need to remember to define on this page the two variables we've used in the header file, $page and $bg.

```
autumn.php

<?
$page = "The Autumn Collection" ;
$bg = "#D0B283" ;
include 'includes/header.php' ;
?>
<H2><? echo "$sitename: $page" ; ?></H2>
Our seasonal speciality is the brown hooded
cagoule.
<BR/> <BR/>
For more info, email <A HREF="mailto:<? echo
$email ; ?>"><? echo $email ; ?></a>.
<? include 'includes/footer.php' ;
```

Finally, there are the closing </BODY> and </HTML> tags, which will also be common to all pages, so we can stick those in an included file called *footer.php* (I know, there's not much point when it's just these two tags, but humour me – the footer could in theory close off a table layout or include a bar of footer links, copyright information, and so on).

```
footer.php
</BODY>
</HTML>
```

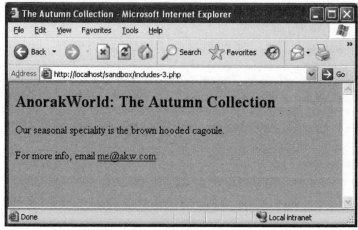

We could now build the Spring Collection page by copying *autumn.php* and editing where necessary. Then both files will draw on the same header and footer files, so we can update the overall page template for both (as well as for Summer, Winter, Kids, HolidayWear, etc.) all at once. But that seems to me like we are straying down the path of lots of repeated code – can we cunningly use the URL to pass some parameters to a generic products page, which will then suck in the appropriate content from included files? Oh yes we can.

Variable includes

Looking at *autumn.php*, we might reasonably decide that only the central line of text is going to differ substantially from any other products page. The rest of the content follows a pattern which we could make into a generic template page which picks up the parameters it needs from the URL. An included file can refer to a variable instead of a fixed filename, so we could re-write the page with a new variable, $inc, which refers to the filename of an included file:

```
<?
$page = array_key_exists('page', $_GET) ?
$_GET['page'] : "Standard" ;
$bg = array_key_exists('bg', $_GET) ?
$_GET['bg'] : "FFFFFF" ;
$inc = array_key_exists('inc', $_GET) ?
$_GET['inc'] : "default" ;
```

Notice how the code uses the ternary operator to define default values if the query string does not supply them.

```
include 'includes/header.php' ;
?>
<H2><? echo "$sitename: The $page Collection" ;
?></H2>
<? include 'includes/' . $inc . '.txt' ; ?>
<BR/> <BR/>
For more info, email <A HREF="mailto: <?echo
$email ; ?>"><?echo $email ; ?></a>.
<? include 'includes/footer.php' ;
```

Now we don't need to create a Spring page at all – we can just write the relevant text into a plain text file called *spring.txt*, and then reference it in the URL along with the title and background colour variables:

```
<A HREF="products.php?page=Spring&bg=93EA69&
inc=spring"
```

Now our page is much closer to the ideal of separating content from structure. By changing just the three template files, we could implement a redesign across three hundred or three thousand pages of content.

6.3 Using functions

A function is a block of pre-written code which produces some kind of output, usually dependent on one or more input variables. There are predefined functions in PHP, such as echo() or substr(), and your own functions are built out of a combination of these functions. They both work in much the same way though, and your functions can use other functions which you have already defined, as well as the predefined ones.

The only real difference is that predefined functions can be used whenever you want, whereas the functions you define yourself must be made available to the page using them, by defining them somewhere in the same page (or via an included file). Another minor difference is that you never actually see the innards of a predefined PHP function, whereas your own functions are explicitly written out in the code.

But in logical terms, a function is a function is a function, whether it was you who defined it or one of those clever people in the PHP development community.

Defining functions

A function has three components which need to be defined: a name, a list of 'arguments' and the code to be executed when the function is called. The function name is needed when the function is called. The input variables for a function are called 'arguments'. They are optional – a function may not require any inputs at all – but if they do exist, they need to be listed in the definition. This is so that the parser knows what inputs to look for when the function is called, and what to do with them. These three components are put together using the following syntax:

```
function function_name($argument1, $argument2) {

    statement(s) to be executed ;

}
```

A simple function with no arguments would look like this:

```php
function say_hi() {
    echo "Hi there!" ;
}
```

A function with some arguments would look like this:

```php
function quote($materials, $time) {
    return ($materials*2) + ($time*12.75) ;
}
```

Use original names!

Since user-defined functions and predefined PHP functions are essentially the same things, used in the same ways, it is important that you don't accidentally give your function a name which is already in use. Given the huge number of predefined functions, this will probably happen to you sooner or later – watch out for error messages like the ones below, and rename your function if necessary. If in doubt, go to www.php.net and search the function list for your proposed name.

```
Fatal error: Cannot redeclare header() in
E:\sandbox\functions.php on line 7
```

```
Parse error: syntax error, unexpected T_ECHO,
expecting T_STRING in E:\sandbox\functions.php
on line 5
```

Note also that as with variables, function names are case-sensitive – if you define a function `foo()` and try to call `Foo()`, it will not work.

Arrays as arguments

As well as using individual variables as arguments for functions, you can supply an entire array as an argument, and make use of the separate elements in the function. Suppose we have an array `$fruit` with three elements: 'name', 'shape' and 'colour'. We could use these in a function `describe_fruit()` like this:

```php
function describe_fruit($fruit) {
    echo "The $fruit[0] is $fruit[1] and
$fruit[2]." ;
}
```

Variable variables

Sometimes it is useful to be able to use a variable whose contents are especially flexible. If the previous example had several arrays like $fruit, each containing details of a different fruit, we could do the following:

```
$banana = array("banana", "crescent-shaped",
"yellow") ;
$apple = array("apple", "round", "green") ;
$fruit = $apple ;
```

We could then call describe_fruit($fruit) and it would describe the apple, because the parser knows that $apple is a variable and should be treated as such. But what happens if we try to pick up the value of $fruit from a query string like grocer.php?fruit=apple?

```
$fruit = $_GET['fruit'] ;
```

We get apple as a string, *not* as the variable $apple. And we can't just concatenate "$" and "apple" to make it into a variable, because the dollar sign might just be part of the string.

To get round this, we need to tell the parser to treat the contents of $fruit as a variable, not a string. To do this, use a double dollar sign instead of the normal single one:

```
describe_fruit($$fruit) ;
```

This says to the parser 'take the contents of $fruit (i.e. apple) and find the variable with that name (i.e. $apple), then use *those* contents (i.e. the contents of the $apple array)'.

Calling functions

Functions are called by just invoking their name, along with any arguments the function needs to work:

```
myFunction($x, $y, $z) ;
```

When a function is called, the parser jumps to the code inside the function and executes it in full before returning to where the function was called from, and then continues reading from there. We could use the functions say_hi() and quote() defined above like this:

```
<?
say_hi();
$t = 3 ;
$m = 25.95 ;
echo "<P>Based on our estimates of time and
materials, the job will cost □" ;
echo quote($m, $t);
echo "<P>Please advise if this is acceptable." ;
?>
```

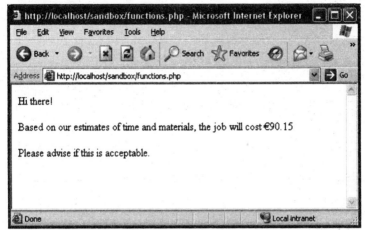

Note two things about how arguments are referred to in these function calls – first, even though there are no arguments required for the say_hi() function, we still have to enclose their non-existence in brackets. Second, we have created the variables $t and $m and used them in the function call. These variable names do not match the argument names. They could be the same if you like – and where possible I try to ensure they are, just to help avoid confusion – but they do not have to be.

Call me whenever you like ...

So far we have seen that code is executed sequentially (except where it branches through control structures), so you might expect to have to define a function before you can use it. In fact that's not necessarily so – if you call a function, the parser will go off and look for a definition. As long as it is defined somewhere in the same page, there is no problem.

```
call_me() ;
function call_me() {
    echo "You can call me any time..." ;
}
```

The exception to this is if your function is 'conditional' – i.e. it is only defined if a certain condition is met. The function `call_me()` below could only be called *after* the parser has reached the `if ($bling >= 1000)` condition and evaluated it to be TRUE.

```
call_me() ;
```

This will not work because the condition below has not been evaluated.

```
if ($bling >= 1000) {
    function call_me() {
        echo "You can only call me if you're bling
    enough" ;
    }
}
call_me() ;
```

This will work, as long as the value of `$bling` is high enough.

Functions with default values

If you write a function which frequently – but not always – uses the same value, it may be convenient to set that value as a default in the function. For instance, suppose you have a VAT calculating function, which normally needs to add VAT at the standard 17.5%, but will occasionally need to use a non-standard rate. If a default value of 17.5% is set for the rate, there's no need to supply it as an argument each time the function is called, unless we specifically want to apply a non-standard VAT rate. To assign a default value to an argument, we just use the equals operator in the argument list:

```
function addvat($total, $rate=17.5) {
    $total += $total * ($rate/100) ;
    return $total;
}
```

Now to call the function using a special rate, we supply both arguments, as with a normal function:

```
echo "<P>Total including discounted VAT = □" .
  addvat(150, 5.5) ;
```

But if we just want to use the standard rate, we only need to supply the $total argument:

```
echo "<P>Total including normal VAT = □" .
  addvat(150) ;
```

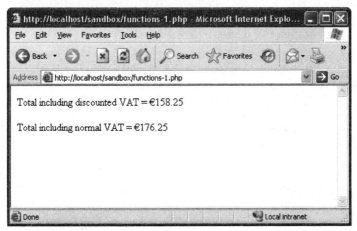

Losing arguments by default!

You need to be a bit careful when playing with default arguments for functions, because they need to be placed in the right order. Any arguments *without* default values should go first in the list, followed by arguments with defaults. If we rewrote the addvat() function as it is below, it would only work as long as both arguments were supplied in the function call – if we actually tried to use the default, it would fail.

```
addvat($rate=17.5, $total)
```

Exercises

1 Look at an HTML site you have worked on recently and copy a few pages into your PHP working area. Look at the structure and try to carve out common chunks of code, then rebuild the pages as PHP file with included files.

   Hint: if you do not have a suitable site to hand, try saving some pages from a favourite site and using them instead.

2 Create a few widget arrays, giving each widget a name, a category and some other properties; save these as a file to be included. Then create stylesheets to alter the appearance of the page based on the different categories (you should have more widgets than categories). Now build a page which picks up the value 'widget' from the query string and uses functions to display a description of the widget in the appropriate style.

Hint: you will need to use a variable variable to get the relevant data out of the widget arrays.

3 Add 'price' and 'weight' elements to the widget arrays, and write a function for the display page which calculates the price including delivery. The shipping costs are €15.25 per kg, but the first kg is always free.

Summary

♦ PHP can be used to increase the efficiency and ease of maintenance of your websites by reusing modular blocks of code.

♦ The `include()` function takes the contents of a separate file and draws it into the calling page.

♦ PHP code in an included file must be enclosed in <? ?> tags in order to execute properly.

♦ Variables defined in the calling page *or* the included file may be used by code in either file.

♦ Functions are processes which can be applied to variable inputs to produce different outputs. PHP has thousands of predefined functions, but you can also create your own new ones.

♦ The variables used by a function are called its arguments; a function can have zero, one or many arguments.

♦ Arguments can have default values which are used if a specific value is not supplied when the function is called.

07

handling forms

In this chapter you will learn:

- how to use PHP to post data via forms
- how to collect and use submitted form data
- how to validate data
- how to display errors for invalid data

7.1 Using PHP to handle forms

There are two display pages associated with handling any form. First, there must be a page which sets up the form so that the user can enter data into it, then there is a page which is displayed after the form has been sent and the data processed in some way. These two functions may be performed by separate scripts, but they are often handled by a single script which uses a control structure to determine whether to display the form or process it. The benefits of this become clear when we start validating the data: with two scripts, if the user enters some bad data, all you can really do is display an error message and send the user back to the form page. With a single script, you can redisplay the form with any bad data clearly flagged up for the user's attention.

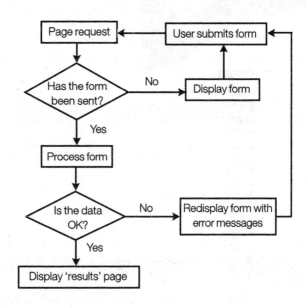

Setting up the form

Creating the form does not have to involve any PHP at all – it can simply be a plain HTML form, with the form's ACTION attribute set to the PHP script which will process the form. We will start by using separate scripts to send and receive the data, so the first script will look something like this:

```
<FORM METHOD="POST" ACTION="formhandler.php">
<P>Your message: <INPUT TYPE="text" NAME="msg" />
<P>Your favourite colour: <SELECT NAME="col">
   <OPTION VALUE="#FF0000">red</OPTION>
   <OPTION VALUE="#00FF00">green</OPTION>
   <OPTION VALUE="#0000FF">blue</OPTION>
</SELECT>
<P><INPUT TYPE="SUBMIT" VALUE="Send" />
</FORM>
```

Processing the form

The data sent via a form consists of name-value pairs: the name of the form field and the value submitted for it. These are stored in a superglobal array called $_POST, and they are accessed in exactly the same way as $_GET data. So to use the data collected by the form above, we could do something like the following:

```
<BODY BGCOLOR="<? echo $_POST['col'] ?>">
<? echo $_POST['msg'] ?>
<P><A HREF="formsender.php">Let's go again!</A>
```

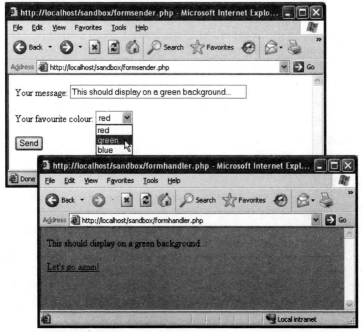

The main difference between them is that $_POST data is cleaner than $_GET data – requiring less messing about to trap possible errors. Assuming you were the person who created the form in the first place, you know exactly what keys exist in the array, and even if the user has failed to fill in all the fields, a value of " " will still have been submitted with each blank field. Moreover, the user cannot interfere by editing the URL query string.

Your first fully interactive page!

Instead of using separate scripts to send and receive the form data, let's combine them into one script.

When using a single script to both send and receive form data, the ACTION will point to itself instead of a second file – perhaps using $_SERVER['PHP_SELF']. So the code dealing with the form display stays much the same.

```
<FORM METHOD="POST" ACTION="<? echo
$_SERVER['PHP_SELF'] ?>">
```

But we can't have the page referring to the posted data until after we are sure that the form has been sent, so we need to build a control structure around the form and the echoed message. The condition to test for is whether the array $_POST exists, because if form data is not posted with a page, there is no $_POST array. The syntax for asking whether a variable exists is simply if ($_POST)...

The two separate pages above can be combined into one like this:

```
<HTML>
<?
if ($_POST) {
?>
    <BODY BGCOLOR="<? echo $_POST['col'] ?>">
    <? echo $_POST['msg'] ?>
    <P><A HREF="<? echo $_SERVER['PHP_SELF']
?>">Let's go again!</A>
<?
} else {
?>
```

```
    <BODY>
    <FORM METHOD="POST" ACTION="<? echo
$_SERVER['PHP_SELF'] ?>">
    <P>Your message: <INPUT TYPE="text" NAME="msg"
size="45" />
    <P>Your favourite colour: <SELECT NAME="col">
       <OPTION VALUE="#FF0000">red</OPTION>
       <OPTION VALUE="#00FF00">green</OPTION>
       <OPTION VALUE="#0000FF">blue</OPTION>
    </SELECT>
    <P><INPUT TYPE="SUBMIT" VALUE="Send" />
    </FORM>
<?
}  ——————[ Don't forget to close the if... else... braces! ]
?>
</BODY>
</HTML>
```

Notice that the code in the <SELECT> block has been indented. Even though we've stepped out of PHP and into HTML, it's still a good idea to maintain the indentation so we can read the code easily.

Hidden fields

Extracting data from hidden form fields is exactly the same process as for visible ones. The $_POST array will hold name-value pairs for any field type – just give it a name and you can get to it. This can be very useful for passing on information which you don't need to display to the user.

7.2 Cleaning and validating data

Before we can be sure that the information sent to us by a form is really useful, we need to know two things:

* Is the data 'clean' – is it in the format you want it? Or does it have rogue characters in like leading spaces which could mess up any alphabetization we might want to do with it? What about single and double quotes – won't they cause problems

when trying to manipulate the data? If you tried the example form above and typed a message into the box which included quotes, you will have noticed that they were automatically escaped. This is essential for accurately inserting data into databases, but it does leave us with backslashes which we don't want to display to the user!

• Is the data valid? Do we have data for all the required fields? If we asked for an e-mail address or phone number, can we perform some basic checks to see whether the data submitted is of the right format?

Cleaning and validating data is an important part of form handling, and to do it properly we will need some more advanced string functions.

More string functions

In Chapter 3 we met the function substr(), which allows us to return a chunk of a given string by specifying the character to start the substring, and its length. In fact, it can also be used to look backwards through the string from the end. This makes it a very useful tool, but it is not sufficient by itself for the kind of cleaning and validating tasks we may be faced with. Here are a few string functions to use when handling form data:

• strlen($str) Returns the number of characters in the string $str

• trim($str) Removes spaces from both ends of $str

• strtolower($str) Converts all characters in $str to lower case.

• strtoupper($str) Converts all characters in $str to upper case.

• nl2br($str) Replaces any new lines in $str with HTML <BR/> tags (useful for displaying long pieces of text from a TEXTAREA input)

• htmlentities($str) Replaces certain characters with their equivalent HTML entities – e.g. < becomes < – useful if you want to display code snippets on screen without them being processed.

• html_entity_decode($str) Performs the reverse of htmlentities($str)

- `strpos($str, $x)` Searches `$str` and returns the first occurrence of `$x` as a number (the nth character of `$str`). If `$x` is not found in `$str`, the function returns FALSE. Case-sensitive.

- `stripos($str, $x)` As above, only the search is NOT case-sensitive.

- `strrpos($str, $x)` Searches `$str` and returns the last occurrence of `$x` as a number. Case-sensitive.

- `strripos($str, $x)` Case-insensitive version of the above.

- `str_replace($x, $y, $str)` Searches `$str` for `$x`, and replaces it with `$y` wherever it occurs. All three can be arrays, so you can search and replace multiple terms in multiple strings. Case-sensitive.

- `str_ireplace($x, $y, $str)` As above, only the search is NOT case-sensitive.

- `stripslashes($str)` Removes backslashes before single and double quotes in `$str`, and replaces double backslashes with single ones (useful for displaying strings which had slashes automatically added).

- `strip_tags($str)` Removes HTML and PHP tags from `$str` (a useful security precaution against hackers trying to insert potentially harmful material into your pages).

- `is_numeric($str)` Returns TRUE if `$str` can be handled as a number.

- `ctype_digit($str)` Returns TRUE if `$str` contains *only* numeric characters. Slightly different to `is_numeric()`, because this will return FALSE if `$str` has a decimal point in it.

- `ctype_alnum($str)` Returns TRUE if `$str` contains *only* alphanumeric characters.

- `ctype_alpha($str)` Returns TRUE if `$str` contains *only* alphabetic characters.

Cleaning form data

Suppose we have a form which collects personal data to build a membership profile for a user. We will want to ensure that we have certain details before we allow an account to be created, and that those details meet certain criteria; for instance, we might want all telephone numbers to consist of digits only – no spaces or brackets, so that we can use an autodialler to call them.

Field	Required?	Constraints
forename	Yes	Must be less than 100 characters
surname	Yes	Must be less than 100 characters
age	No	Must be a number
sex	No	M or F
email	Yes	Must have an @ and at least one dot in it; the last dot must come after the @; must not contain any spaces
tel	No	Integers only – no spaces or brackets
biog	No	Must be less than 1000 characters

We can ensure that some of these constraints are met using HTML attributes in the form fields – for instance, we can use the MAXLENGTH attribute on the name text inputs to prevent stupidly long names being entered; radio buttons with values set to M and F for sex. The rest will have to be dealt with at the server using PHP.

A good starting point is to take the $_POST array and turn it into a set of separate variables. This gives us nice neat variable names we can manipulate to our hearts' content without having to fiddle about with awkward-to-type terms like $_POST['forename']. We can do this by running a foreach... loop through the array, and assigning the form's name–value pairs to named variables (using the field names as variable variables – see page 92):

```
foreach($_POST as $fn => $v) {
    $$fn = $v ;
}
```

While we're at it, some basic cleaning won't hurt – we can strip out any leading or trailing spaces using trim():

```
foreach($_POST as $fn => $v) {
    $v = trim($v) ;
    $$fn = $v ;
}
```

This provides us with the variables $forename, $surname, $age, $sex, $email, $tel and $biog, together with trimmed values. We need to do some validation on the $age and $email data, but first let's do some basic cleaning.

First, the telephone number should have any odd brackets or spaces removed. Create an array containing the characters you might want to strip out, then use str_replace() to replace these with nothing (""):

```
$notel = array(" ", "(", ")", "[", "]", "-",
".", ",", "#") ;
$tel = str_replace($notel, "", $tel) ;
```

There is one non-numeric character in a phone number which we should not ignore – a + symbol indicates an international dialling code which the autodialler will need to know. We could perform another str_replace() on the stripped-down $tel, or we could use a more compact solution. When arrays are used as search and replace variables, the parser goes through the string taking each element of the search array and replacing it with the corresponding element in the replace array. If there are more search terms than replace terms, the remaining search elements are replaced with a blank value, i.e. they are simply cut. This means that we can add the + symbol to the $notel array, and use an array with just one element ("00") for the replace argument:

```
$notel = array("+", " ", "(", ")", "[", "]", "-
", ".", ",", "#") ;
$tel = str_replace($notel, array("00"), $tel) ;
```

The parser replaces the + with a double zero, and then goes through the rest of the search terms replacing them with nothing. We should now be left with a clean number – but we will check it anyway, just to make sure!

Second, if we want to display the user's self-description given in $biog then we should subject it to the stripslashes() function, just in case there are any escape characters in it. This is easy:

```
$biog = stripslashes($biog) ;
```

Validation

The first piece of validation we need to do is to make sure that no required fields were left blank. We will need a variable called $error to display any error messages, too.

```
$error = "" ;
if (($forename == "") ||
    ($surname == "") ||
    ($email == "")) {
   $error = "Please fill in all the required
      fields.<BR/>" ;
}
```

To establish whether $age is really a number (we want this rather than a text value so that in future we can analyse our data by age group), we can use is_numeric():

```
if (is_numeric($age) == FALSE) {
   $error .= "Please enter a valid age (numbers
only!)" ;
}
```

Notice that the error message here is being appended to the existing value of $error so that we don't lose any previous error message(s). After we have finished validating all the data we can check the value of $error; if it is blank, everything is OK, otherwise we display the error messages.

We can use the same check for the telephone number – the is_numeric() function will return TRUE even if the number starts with some leading zeroes. Now we need to check $email for some characteristic signs of a valid address, using strpos() and strrpos(). First, make sure that there is an @ symbol and at least one dot.

```
if ((strpos($email, "@") === FALSE) ||
    (strpos($email, ".") === FALSE)) {
   $error .= "Please enter a valid email address"
   ;
}
```

Now add another condition to make sure there is no whitespace in the address:

```
(strpos($email, " ") != FALSE)
```

How many 'equals' equals 'equal'?

Notice that in the e-mail validation the triple equals sign is used to check for a FALSE condition. This is because a Boolean FALSE can also be written as 0, and strpos() can return a zero if the search term is found at the 0th (first) character of the string. Only the triple equals can distinguish between the two results. In fact, in this particular case, we might be better off using the double equals instead of the triple, because any e-mail address starting with an @ is not right! But you should be aware of the distinction, otherwise it will be one of those 'gotchas' which may one day cause you hours of painful debugging to identify.

The final check is to see whether there is a dot after the @. We will do this by comparing the position of the @ with the position of the *last* dot. If it is greater – i.e. further to the right – we know we have a bad e-mail address, so we can add this condition to the list:

```
(strpos($email, "@") > strrpos($email, "."))
```

So the complete set of conditions looks like this:

```
if ((strpos($email, "@") === FALSE) ||
    (strpos($email, ".") === FALSE) ||
    (strpos($email, " ") != FALSE) ||
    (strpos($email, "@") > strrpos($email,
".")))  {
    $error = "Please enter a valid email address"
;
}
```

This validation will not completely prevent people from submitting mistaken or made-up e-mail addresses. The only way to be sure you have a user's real address is to force them to reply to a mail sent there (and even then, there is nothing to stop someone signing up with a free e-mail service). In fact, probably the easiest way to get sensible e-mail addresses is just to ask for it twice and compare the results (if ($email1 != $email2)...). This will ferret out any mistyping more effectively than the conditions set out above. However, this kind of validation *could* trap some errors – and more to the point, it has allowed me to explain some more useful string functions!

7.3 Putting it all together

Before we show the full script for this example, it's worth a quick look at the structure using some pseudocode:

```php
<?
// if the form has been posted, analyse it:
if ($_POST) {
    foreach($_POST as $k => $v) {
        $v = trim($v) ;
        $$k = $v ;
    }
    $error = "" ;
    // cleaning and validation code here...
    // ...then display errors or results:
    if ($error != "") {
        echo "$error <P>Please try again." ;
    } else {
        echo "<P><B>Forename:</B> $forename<BR/>" ;
        // etc...
    }
// if the form has not been posted, display it!
} else {
?>
    <FORM METHOD="POST" ACTION="<? echo
$_SERVER['PHP_SELF'] ?>">
    <!- HTML to display form ->
<?
// remember to close the if... braces!
}
?>
```

Now for the full code listing:

```html
<HTML>
<HEAD>
<LINK REL="stylesheet" TYPE="text/css"
HREF="plain.css" />
</HEAD>
<BODY>
<?
if ($_POST) {
    foreach($_POST as $k => $v) {
        $v = trim($v) ;
```

```
      $$k = $v ;
   }

   // create empty error variable
   $error = "" ;

   // check for data in required fields
   if (($forename == "") ||
       ($surname == "") ||
       ($email == "")) {
      $error = "Please fill in all the required
fields.<BR/>" ;
   }

   // validate $age
   if (is_numeric($age) == FALSE) {
      $error = "Please enter a valid age (numbers
only!)<BR/>" ;
   }

   // validate $email
   if ((strpos($email, "@") === FALSE) ||
       (strpos($email, ".") === FALSE) ||
       (strpos($email, " ") != FALSE) ||
       (strpos($email, "@") > strrpos($email,
".")))) {
      $error .= "Please enter a valid email
address<BR/>" ;
   }

   // clean and validate $tel
   $notel = array("+", " ", "(", ")", "[", "]",
"-", ",", "#") ;
   $tel = str_replace($notel, array("00"), $tel)
;
   if (is_numeric($tel)== FALSE) {
      $error .= "Please enter a valid telephone
number<BR/>" ;
   }

   // clean $biog and add <br/>s
   $biog = stripslashes($biog) ;
```

```
    $biog = nl2br($biog) ;

    if ($error != "") {
       echo "$error <P>Please hit the back button
to try again." ;
    } else {
       echo "<P><B>Forename:</B> $forename<BR/>" ;
       echo "<B>Surname:</B> $surname<BR/>" ;
       echo "<B>Age:</B> $age<BR/>" ;
       echo "<B>Sex:</B> $sex<BR/>" ;
       echo "<B>Email:</B> $email<BR/>" ;
       echo "<B>Telephone:</B> $tel<BR/>" ;
       echo "<B>Description:</B> $biog<BR/>" ;
    }

} else {

?>
    <TABLE BORDER="0" CELLPADDING="3"
CELLSPACING="0">
    <FORM METHOD="POST" ACTION="<? echo
$_SERVER['PHP_SELF'] ?>">
    <TR
       <TD>Forename:</TD>
       <TD><INPUT TYPE="text" NAME="forename"
SIZE="45" MAXLENGTH="100"/></TD>
    </TR><TR>
       <TD>Surname:</TD>
       <TD><INPUT TYPE="text" NAME="surname"
SIZE="45" MAXLENGTH="100"/></TD>
    </TR><TR>
       <TD>Age:</TD>
       <TD><INPUT TYPE="text" NAME="age" SIZE="5"
MAXLENGTH="5"/></TD>
    </TR><TR>
       <TD>Sex:</TD>
       <TD><INPUT TYPE="radio" NAME="sex"
VALUE="F"/>F
          <INPUT TYPE="radio" NAME="sex"
VALUE="M"/>M</TD>
    </TR><TR>
       <TD>Email:</TD>
```

```
        <TD><INPUT TYPE="text" NAME="email"
SIZE="45" MAXLENGTH="100"/></TD>
    </TR><TR>
        <TD>Telephone:</TD>
        <TD><INPUT TYPE="text" NAME="tel" SIZE="45"
MAXLENGTH="20"/></TD>
    </TR><TR>
        <TD COLSPAN="2">Describe yourself in a few
words:</TD>
    </TR><TR>
        <TD COLSPAN="2"><TEXTAREA NAME="biog"
ROWS="4" COLS="47"></TEXTAREA></TD>
    </TR><TR>
        <TD COLSPAN="2"><INPUT TYPE="SUBMIT"
VALUE="Send" /></TD>
    </TR>
    </FORM>
    </TABLE>
<?
}
?>
</BODY>
</HTML>
```

7.4 Displaying helpful error messages

It is all very well validating the data and displaying an error message on the results page saying "Hey idiot! You got this bit wrong! Hit the Back button and try again!" But wouldn't it be nicer if our forms could be more helpful? Even clever people can do really stupid stuff sometimes and you don't want to be too judgemental, do you? You do? Oh. Well in that case, skip on a few pages. Otherwise read on ...

Ideally, a form with invalid data should be redisplayed, with the problem fields clearly flagged, and all submitted data dropped into the right places. This means taking the form display code outside the if ($_POST) control structure, and writing a new control structure which displays the form if *either* the form has not been posted, *or* it has been posted, but there are errors:

```
if (!$_POST) || ($error != "")...
```

Displaying data in the form

This is easy enough for text inputs – we just drop the data into the form using the VALUE attribute of each field:

```
<INPUT TYPE="text" NAME="age" VALUE="<? echo
$age ?>" />
```

To reproduce the user's selections from drop-down menus, checkboxes and radio buttons, we need to be slightly more cunning and use control structures to determine which field gets the SELECTED or CHECKED attribute. For instance, to handle the $sex radio buttons, we would need to add some variables to the form code:

```
<INPUT TYPE="radio" NAME="sex" VALUE="F" <? echo
$sexf_sel ?> />

<INPUT TYPE="radio" NAME="sex" VALUE="M" <? echo
$sexm_sel ?> />
```

Then we can check the value of $sex and assign the value CHECKED to the appropriate variable, leaving the other one blank:

```
$sexf_sel = $sexm_sel = "" ;
if ($sex =="F") {
   $sexm_sel = "CHECKED" ;
} elseif ($sex =="M") {
   $sexf_sel = "CHECKED" ;
}
```

The same method works for menus and checkboxes, using SELECTED for the selected <OPTION>, and CHECKED for any active checkboxes.

Highlighting error messages

Flagging up a field for attention means we need to do something similar to the approach above. We can add a variable next to each field which is blank by default, but can be assigned a value if necessary. This could display an error message, an asterisk or a graphical mark of some sort. If there is no problem with the form content, nothing is shown, but when required, the error variables come into play. Alternatively you could use the variables to change the style of those form fields which require the user's attention:

```
<STYLE TYPE="text/css">
.error {border: 1px solid #FF0000; background-
color: #DDDDFF;}
</STYLE>
<?
// create default (empty) variables
$forename_x = $surname_x = $age_x = $email_x =
$tel_x = "" ;

// test for error conditions
if ($forename == "") {
   $forename_x = "error" ;
}
...etc
<TR>
   <TD>Forename:</TD>
   <TD><INPUT TYPE="text" NAME="forename"
VALUE="<? echo $forename ?>" CLASS="<? echo
$forename_x ?>" /></TD>
</TR>
...etc
```

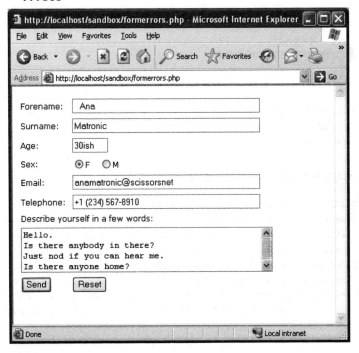

Form reset buttons

You are probably used to using the RESET button on HTML forms to clear the fields and allow the user to start again. However, the button doesn't actually clear the fields – it resets them to the values they had when the page was loaded. This means that if you have been using PHP to insert values into the form, the RESET button will simply reset the form to the state it was in when it was last submitted – not to blank fields. If you want a button to clear fields, you will need to use some client-side scripting or provide a link to reload the page.

```
<INPUT TYPE="button" VALUE="Clear Fields"
onClick="location.href='<? echo
$_SERVER['PHP_SELF'] ?>';" />
```

Exercises

1 Write a script for an online quote generator for a car hire firm. It displays a form requesting information from the potential customer about their requirements, then processes the form to quote a price. Include a variety of vehicles and optional extras, as well as the duration of the hire and the customer's name, contact telephone and e-mail.

2 Build in some validation so that the customer must fill in all fields except the optional extras. Clean the telephone number to remove non-numeric characters and perform some basic validation to check that the e-mail address is good.

3 After a successful quote, provide a "quote again" button which redisplays the form with the customer's details preserved, but the other fields cleared.

Hint: to stop error messages showing when you do this, include an extra variable as a hidden input, and use it to decide which parts of the form to validate.

Summary

*   Using PHP to handle forms enables you to get the right data in the right format. Data can be cleaned and validated according to complex rules, and users can be clearly shown where they need to amend their entries.

*   Form-handling scripts can be separate from the form code itself, or both can be incorporated into a single script using appropriate control structures.

*   PHP has numerous functions for analysing and manipulating strings, which are used to clean and validate form data.

*   To redisplay some kinds of submitted data in a form (radio buttons and drop-down menus, for instance), you will need to create new variables to mark the selected form element.

*   It is useful to display error flags against fields which require the user's attention: create variables which are empty by default, but which can be assigned a value if necessary.

08

sessions and cookies

In this chapter you will learn:

- about browser sessions
- how to store and use session variables
- about cookies
- how to store and use cookies
- how to set HTTP headers

8.1 Session variables and cookies

When web page information is transmitted between a web server and a browser, it is sent via a protocol called HyperText Transfer Protocol – HTTP. This protocol is said to be 'stateless' – which basically means that a web server has no long-term memory. Every time it receives a page request it makes no connection with any previous requests. A user may have spent half an hour clicking their way round a site, sending hundreds of page requests to the server, but every time they will get the same 'blank look' from the server as if they were a user who has never been there before.

This is inconvenient for web developers who frequently want to retain information about a user as they hop around their site, or even between visits. There are two kinds of tool for storing and retrieving such information: 'session variables' and 'cookies'. The two are closely related – in fact session variables are often stored with the help of a cookie – but let's draw a slightly artificial line between them for the moment.

Information stored in a session variable exists for a limited period, generally until the user closes their browser. Cookies may still be retrievable at a later session – days, weeks or even years later. However, cookies can be refused by users, whereas session variables can to an extent circumvent this restriction.

Cookies

You are probably familiar with cookies – small files stored on the user's computer containing snippets of information which in one way or another help identify them to your website. If you are a Windows user, have a look in the Cookies folder (under Documents and Settings, then your username) – try opening one in a text editor and you will see something like this:

```
SITEID
2238974siudf
www.somewebsite.com/
*
```

The first two lines are a name–value pair which store the data actually retrieved when the cookie is read, and the third shows which domain issued the cookie. This is a simple example, and many cookies have extra bits of content as well, but this gives us what we need to know for now.

When you set a cookie, you determine the name and value to be stored, and you can optionally set an EXPIRE parameter, which sets the length of time before the cookie is rendered inactive. By default, this is 0, which means it expires as soon as the browser is closed.

Cookie controversy

There is some controversy surrounding the use of cookies. This is partly on privacy grounds – cookies could be used to store information about a user's browsing habits without them agreeing to it, and could then be linked to information which identifies them personally. It is also debatable as to whether a website should have the right to help themselves to the use of somebody else's hard disk.

Some kinds of functionality really do require the use of a cookie, and the fact that browsers are generally set up to receive cookies reflects the fact that it is usually in the user's interests to let you write small files to their disk (though most browsers limit the number of cookies they will accept from any given site).

If you want to use cookies to track users' behaviour for your own benefit, you should ensure you have a clear privacy policy on the site explaining what you will and will not use the information for. If you are storing any kind of personally identifying information about a user, you may also be legally obliged to take certain measures regarding data protection.

Session variables

A session variable is, as you might guess from the title, a more temporary solution than a cookie. It is a variable which is stored and can only be used for the lifetime of a 'session' that the user spends at your site. Of course there are problems with defining this period of time, since the server can't tell the difference between a request from one user and one from another. How can we know anything useful about a user on your site without using a cookie to identify them?

Since HTTP is stateless, the only other way to maintain any kind of 'memory' about a particular user making his or her way around your site would be to incorporate the information into every page request. That means appending the variables as name–value pairs to every `HREF` tag (`<A HREF="mypage.php?user=lucie&clicks=7">`, etc.) and hidden inputs in every form submission.

This is a fiddly task at best, and not 100% effective even if you do code up every single instance. A user only has to visit one page on another site in the middle of a session at your site for that information to get dropped. Even without leaving your site, they could manually type in the address of another page or follow a bookmark – and in both cases they would lose information about the current session. Furthermore, they might bookmark a URL which includes session variables, or send a link to a friend. When the bookmark or link is followed some time later, that information may be completely inappropriate.

Where possible, PHP uses a cookie to determine when a session is over, because it is clearly the easiest and most reliable way of identifying a given user. But where users have browsers which are set to reject cookies, there is a back-up mechanism, which passes on some information with every page request.

This process does not happen in the same way as the manual addition of variables to links and forms. The actual variables are stored in a file on the server, identified by an ID field. This ID field is passed along with every page request and form submission, as part of the HTTP header. It is not in the URL or as a hidden input, so cannot be seen or tampered with by the user.

It is still no guarantee that the information will last a full session, but at least it saves you from having to manipulate a ton of link and form code by hand. It also prevents users from messing about with the information in URL query strings, or accidentally passing on their session information in links and bookmarks.

8.2 Using cookies

Using cookies is actually very straightforward – there is just one function used to set a cookie, and they are retrieved via a superglobal array. However, there are a couple of 'gotchas' to watch out for – one when setting and one when retrieving a cookie – so make sure you read the Gotcha! sections below.

Setting cookies

There are six possible arguments to the setcookie()function, but you will normally only need the first two or three:

```
setcookie('name', 'value', expire)
```

The first two arguments assign the variable's name and value. The third (optional) argument tells the browser how long it should keep the cookie after the end of the session. The expire argument defaults to 0, which means the cookie expires immediately after all browser windows are closed.

So if we are just interested in storing information about a user's current session, we can set a cookie like this:

```
setcookie('user_id', '1f6')
```

Gotcha!

Cookies are handled as part of the HTTP header, so you must set them before any HTML is written, including whitespace or empty lines. Any such output marks the end of the header, and once the header is sent, you cannot go back and add anything to it. If you try to set a cookie after this point, you will get an error message.

When setting cookies, make sure the very first characters in your code are <? and that you set the cookie before you output anything in HTML, even via an echo() or print() statement. Be especially careful when including other files before a call to setcookie(), as they may have some non-header output in them.

Long-term cookies

If you want to store a cookie variable for longer (for instance, to prevent a user voting multiple times during a given period), you will need to set an expiry time. This needs to be given as a *Unix timestamp*, which sounds scarier than it is. If you want to know the details, read the following section about Geek time; otherwise just use the expression below, replacing `integer` with the number of seconds from now until the expiry time:

```
setcookie('has_voted', '1', time() + integer)
```

Rather than get tied up trying to work out how many seconds there are between now and next Tuesday, it is often written as an expression to break down the seconds into minutes, hours, days, etc. For instance, three hours from now would be:

```
setcookie('has_voted', '1', time() + (60 * 60 * 3))
```

And two weeks from now would be:

```
setcookie('has_voted', '1', time() + (60 * 60 * 24 * 7 * 2))
```

Geek time

The Unix timestamp is how computers generally tell the time (whether they are Unix or Windows, in fact). It is basically a long number – the number of seconds which have elapsed since midnight GMT on January 1st 1970 (the beginning of the 'Unix epoch').

For instance, the timestamp 1106744583 translates to Wednesday Jan 26th 2005, 13:03:03 GMT. Surprisingly, this huge number (about 1.1 billion at present) does not get out of hand – there are roughly 31,536,000 (31.5m) seconds in a year, so even two hundred years from now, the Unix timestamp will still only need the same number of digits – it will be about 7.4bn, or 7,413,944,583.

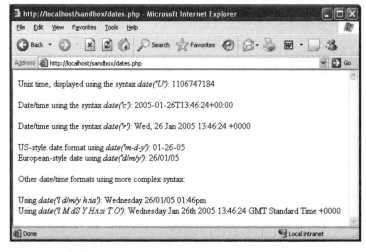

The function `time()` returns the current Unix timestamp, and is the best thing to use if you are passing the time to another program or function. If you want a more human-friendly date/time format, there are alternative functions, such as `date()`, which returns the current date and time in your time zone.

You will need to tell the parser how you want it formatted – for instance, do you want the US-style date 01-26-05 or the European-style 26/01/05?

Look `date()` up in the function list at www.php.net for full details on how to format the date and time in different ways.

Retrieving cookies

If a cookie issued by your site exists on a user's computer when they request one of your pages, its contents are automatically read and stored in the superglobal array `$_COOKIE`. So to retrieve the value of a cookie variable you just use the syntax `$_COOKIE['variable_name']`. To retrieve the cookie we set in the code above:

```
$user_id = $_COOKIE['user_id'];
echo "User ID is $user_id";
```

And the output of this would be:

```
User ID is 1f6
```

When a page sets a cookie, the cookie is not added to the superglobal array until the next time the user requests a page. This means that you cannot set a cookie at the top of a page and then refer to its value via `$_COOKIE['name']` later on in the same page.

If you think about it, this actually makes perfect sense – if you have a cookie which determines whether this is a user's first visit to a certain page, you don't want it to take effect until *after* the user has visited the page for the first time. And if you do want to refer to the value of a cookie variable, you must already have it available in some form in order to set it, so you don't actually need to retrieve it from the cookie.

Editing cookies

Once a cookie has been set, you can change its value at any time simply by resetting it. Suppose you have a cookie which keeps track of a user's score in a quiz – as he or she progresses through the pages of questions, you will want to update this value a number of times. Each time you want to do this, just call setcookie() again, using the same name but changing the value. So after the first page of questions is submitted, you might have a function which calculates the score $score_1, which you store in a cookie like this:

```
setcookie('score', $score_1)
```

After the next page you would calculate the score from the next batch of questions ($score_2) and update the cookie like this:

```
$current_score = $_COOKIE['score']
setcookie('score', ($current_score + $score_2))
```

Deleting cookies

Since you can only store a limited number of cookies on any given user's machine, it is good practice to get rid of old cookies when you are finished with them. This frees up a cookie space in case you need it for some other information later. Besides, you are helping yourself to someone else's disk, remember, so it is only polite to clean up after yourself.

To delete a cookie, we use setcookie() again, but this time we set the value to an empty value.

```
setcookie('score','')
```

Multiple cookies

To avoid the worst abuses of the cookie privilege – of being allowed to write to a user's hard disk – most browsers set a limit to the number of cookies which can be issued from any given website (as determined by its domain name). Up to that limit, you can set more than one cookie, and they do not all have to have the same expiry time. You might want a fairly permanent user ID cookie, for example, and another one which records any purchases made by the user in the last 30 days. You might also then set some kind of session cookie which expires in a matter of minutes.

For instance, imagine we have a login function which takes a username and password from a user to grant them access to the site. To prevent unauthorized use of the user's login by someone else, we decide to put a timeout on their use of the site. Let's say if they do not request a page at least once every ten minutes, we assume they have left their desk, and we should deny access without re-entering the password.

When the user first logs in, we can set a user ID cookie. We'll set a long expiry time on this, so that if the user returns at a later date, the site recognizes them and just asks for their password.

```
setcookie('UID', 'Bob', time() + (60 * 60 * 24 * 365));
```

We'll also set a timeout cookie, which expires after ten minutes. This doesn't need a value, as we'll only be checking for its existence when deciding whether or not to allow the user to proceed, or whether to prompt for password re-entry.

```
setcookie('timeout', '1', time() + (10*60));
```

Then at the top of every page we can include a function which checks for the existence of the timeout cookie. If it exists, we'll reset it for another ten minutes; if not, we'll prompt the user to log in again. In Chapter 5 we used array_key_exists() to test whether an array element exists or not. The same could be used here, or we can use an alternative, IsSet(). This function can be used on any variable type, not just arrays.

```
if (IsSet($_COOKIE['timeout'])) {
setcookie('timeout', '1', time() + (10*60));
} else {
print "Sorry $UID, your session has timed out.
";
print "Please re-enter your password to con-
tinue";
}
```

Then we would provide a password form, which might include a hidden field to hold a reference for the page the user was trying to view. This way, if they successfully enter their password we know where to send them, instead of just dumping them back at the welcome page.

8.3 Using session variables

If we only want to keep track of a user for the duration of a particular session, the simplest solution is to use PHP's built-in session functions. By using these, we don't have to worry about whether the user's browser is set to accept cookies, and we don't have to go through the laborious task of incorporating variables into every link and form.

The PHP engine will work out what is best and do it for you – all you have to do is tell it to 'start' a session, then feed it variables and pick them up as required. You can also 'destroy' a session and all its variables, but this is not necessary, as this happens when a normal browser session ends anyway.

To start a session, call the function `session_start()`, which checks to see whether a session is currently in progress. If not, then it creates the superglobal array `$_SESSION` which can now be used to store any variables you want to pass between pages. It also creates a 'session identifier' which references the current user's session. If a current session is detected (because you have called `session_start()` on a previous page), then any variables stored with the current session identifier are retrieved and made available via the `$_SESSION` array.

Start sessions often and early!

`session_start()` must be called on any page where you want to make use of session variables. You have to make the PHP engine aware of your intended use of session variables before they can be made available.

Moreover, the session identifier is sent as part of the HTTP header, so the call to `session_start()` must be made *before* any HTML output is written. The same warnings about whitespace, empty lines and included files apply in the same way here as with setting cookies (see the Gotcha! note on page 120).

You can never start a session too early, so if you want to use session variables on a page, stick a `<? session_start(); ?>` right at the top of the script before anything else at all.

Setting and retrieving session variables

Since we are leaving PHP to decide how to actually handle session variables – and since we're not interested in setting an expiry time – the process of setting and retrieving them is really as simple as making up a name for the variable and assigning it a value.

In the first page below we create the variable $_SESSION['user'] and assign it a value. Then in the next page we create the variable $stored_username and assign it the value retrieved from $_SESSION['user']. On both pages we must make the PHP engine aware of our use of session variables by calling session_start() before we try to use them.

```
First page
<?
session_start();
$username = "Lancelot";
$_SESSION['user'] = $username;
?>

Second page
<?
session_start();
$stored_username = $_SESSION['user'];
?>
```

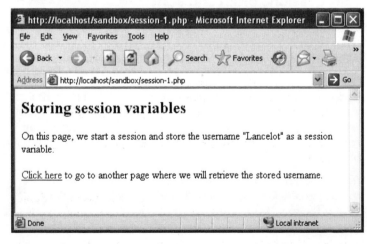

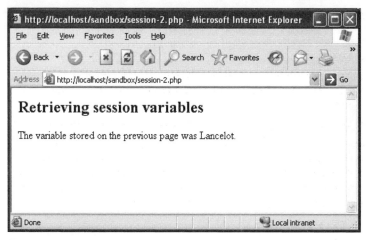

Retrieving session variables

The variable stored on the previous page was Lancelot.

Error-trapping

You need to be careful whenever you are dealing with variables
which are not defined in the script of the current page. As with
other superglobal arrays like $_GET and $_POST, you ought to
build in some error-trapping to handle situations where the cookie
or session variable does not exist.

Are you absolutely certain that a variable has been defined at the
point where you are about to use it? Can you guarantee that the
user has already visited the page which defines it? Are you sure
that a cookie has not expired, and that the user cannot have
deleted it? If the answer to any of these is 'No', you need to
include some conditional statements which can deal with the
situation gracefully instead of exposing an error to your users.

```
if (IsSet($_COOKIE['user_id'])) {
$user_id = $_COOKIE['user_id'];
   echo "Hi $user_id, nice to see you again.";
} else {
   echo "First time here? Let me show you
around...";
}
```

The example below does a similar check for a session variable,
but this time instead of outputting the result text directly, it is
assigned to a variable $score_msg which can be used later on in
the script. This is often a neater approach as you do not have to
nest big chunks of HTML display code inside your PHP logic.

```php
if (IsSet($_SESSION['score'])) {
   $total_score = $_SESSION['score'] +
      $this_score;
   $score_msg = "Your score so far is " .
      $total_score;
   $_SESSION['score'] = $total_score;
} else {
   $score_msg = "Warning! You have arrived at
   section 3 of the quiz, but unfortunately your
   score from previous sections is unavailable.
   You may continue anyway if you want, or <A
   HREF='quiz-1.php'>click here</A> to start
   over.";
}
[...]
echo $score_msg;
```

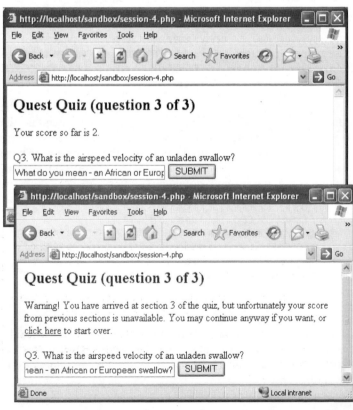

Exercises

1 Use cookies to store a user's name (input via a form), and a Unix timestamp of the moment when it was submitted. Write another script which checks for these cookies. If they are not set, display a welcome message; if they are set, welcome the user back and say how long it has been since their last visit.

2 Use session variables to write a quiz script. The quiz should present questions one by one; the user answers them and a running score is kept. At the end of the quiz, give feedback on whether they have 'passed' or 'failed' the quiz, depending on how many answers they got right.

3 Now add a final link or button to the quiz which allows the user to take the quiz again, resetting their scores.

Summary

- The HTTP protocol used to transfer web page data is 'stateless', meaning that a web server has no idea who it is sending a page to, or whether a series of page requests are in any way related to a particular user.

- To provide a more joined-up experience for users, web developers have two ways of getting around this limitation: cookies and session variables.

- Cookies store variables on a user's computer. Their duration there can be controlled to some extent by setting an expiry time, but the user can edit or delete them, or even block them in the first place.

- In PHP, session variables are stored on the server, with a session identifier. This is stored as a cookie or passed on via HTTP headers, depending on what PHP determines is the best method in the circumstances.

- Session and cookie variables are accessed via the superglobal arrays $_SESSION and $_COOKIE.

- Sessions must be started and cookies must be set as early as possible in your script – *before* any HTML output is written, because they are handled in the HTTP header.

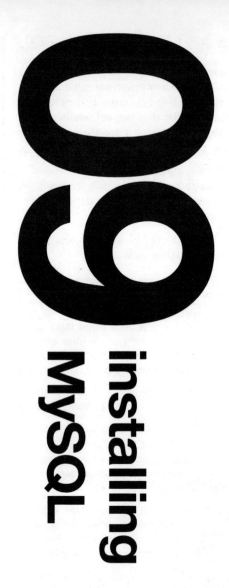

09 installing MySQL

In this chapter you will learn:

- how to download and install MySQL

- how to configure MySQL and PHP to work together

9.1 Downloading and installing MySQL

First of all, you will need to get hold of a copy of the latest version of MySQL. Recent versions of MySQL are available in a nice 'Essentials' package which includes only the files needed to run MySQL on a Windows PC. Older versions came with a host of additional files which were only of use to open-source developers working on the actual MySQL code itself. The Essentials package also comes with a self-installer, making set-up a breeze.

1 Go to http://dev.mysql.com/downloads and look in the **MySQL database server and standard clients** section.

2 Click on the link to the **recommended** version of the software (MySQL 4.1 at the time of writing) and scroll down to the Windows section.

   NOTE: please see the note on Improved MySQL and web hosting on page 137 below before you download this version!

3 Find the **Windows Essentials** section and click on the **Pick a mirror** link to choose a download site.

4 The next page is a form asking for information about you and your intended use of the software. This is optional, and you can skip straight to the download area if you want.

5 You will now see a list of download mirror sites, starting with those which are probably closest to you. Pick one and click the **HTTP** or **FTP** link, and then save the file somewhere safe.

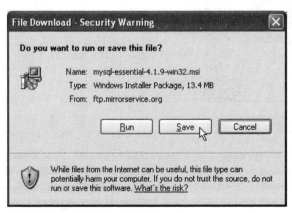

Providing information when downloading

The form asking you about you and your use of MySQL is optional, but it is helpful for the developers. Since they're making MySQL available to you for no charge, it would be churlish not to return the favour in some small way.

However, you can still skip it at this stage without feeling guilty – when you install the software, you will be given the option of registering for a mysql.com account, which comprises much the same information. As a registered member, you have certain site privileges such as adding comments to the online manual or reporting bugs.

Verifying the software

As with your PHP and Apache downloads, the chances that you will find anything other than the genuine MySQL code here are extremely slim. But it never hurts to check, so you should verify that your download is the real thing by using an MD5 checksum (see page 14).

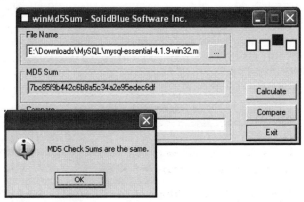

Installing MySQL

If you are working on a Windows platform and have downloaded the Essentials package, installation is very simple. Find your download (called something like **mysql-essential-4.1.9-win32.msi**) and double-click to run. If you have Windows XP you may see a security message such as this:

Just click **Run** – if your MD5 checksum showed that you have a genuine copy of MySQL, then you have nothing to fear. Now follow the installation wizard through, step by step.

When prompted for the type of installation, select **Typical**, then on the next screen, click **Install** to start. If you did not provide any personal information when downloading, you can do so now by registering for a mysql.com account (see note above).

Finally, make sure the **Configure the MySQL Server now** box is checked, and click **Finish** to start the configuration wizard.

The configuration wizard

If you are good with hardware and a seasoned database administrator, you may want to go for the **Detailed Configuration** option. This gives you control over exactly how and where the database is set up, what disk space, memory and CPU usage it can use, whether it should be optimized for applications requiring a transactional database or not, and so on.

If that sounds daunting, go for the **Standard Configuration** option instead. This will give you a general all-purpose database suitable for development, and if at a later date you feel up to taking on the advanced settings, you can do so manually.

1 Leave the default setting **Install As Windows Service**, but check the **Include Bin Directory in Windows PATH** option – this will be useful for working with the database from the command line, in true MySQL style.

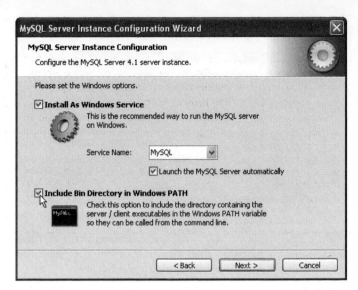

2 Choose a password for the 'root' user (this is a Unix term for the administrator login, i.e. one with all privileges). Make a note of this password and don't lose it – you'll need it every time you want to use the database!

3 Click **Execute** to let the wizard complete the configuration tasks, and then **Finish** when it is all done.

Problems with Firewalls

You may find that you get an error message telling you that there was a problem with the configuration, such as the security settings not being applied. This is probably due to over-zealous personal firewall software such as Norton Internet Security or the Windows Firewall. You may need to adjust your firewall settings to allow the wizard to complete the set-up properly.

Details of what you need to do should be supplied in the error message (for example. "open the TCP port 3006"). You will need to refer to the documentation for your firewall to find out how to do this.

A quick check

Often when you install a program, it is launched when you complete the installation, and you can have a little look round your new toy. But since the MySQL server runs in the background, there is nothing really to see. If, like me, you like to *see* something to know that it's there, try this:

1   Go to the Windows **Start** menu and select **All Programs -> MySQL -> MySQL Server 4.1 -> MySQL Command Line Client.**

2   This opens a command-line window, prompting you for a password. Enter the root password you set during configuration and hit [Return].

3   Type SHOW DATABASES; (including the semicolon) and hit [Return].

If all is well, you should see a table showing the databases currently set up. There will be one called *mysql* which holds basic system data such as usernames and privileges. The other is called test and is empty by default – it seems to be there just so you can practise messing around with a database.

4   To quit the command line window, type exit and hit [Return].

9.2 Additional configuration for PHP

Installing PHP 5 using the Windows installer makes life nice and easy for getting started with PHP, but it does not include everything you need to make it work with the MySQL database. If you've leapt ahead and started trying to connect to the database using PHP, you may have noticed error messages like this:

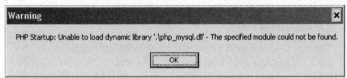

In PHP version 5 and above, MySQL is no longer bundled as part of the standard installation. You will need to download and install some additional material and tinker with the configuration file again to enable the two to work together.

1 Go back to the PHP downloads page at http://www.php.net/downloads.php and scroll down to the section headed PHP 5.0.2 (remember, the version number will probably have changed since the time of writing).

2 This time, download the PHP 5.0.2 zip package, save it and verify it using the MD5 checksum.

3 Open the zip file and extract the following files to your **C:/ PHP directory**: php5ts.dll, php_mysql.dll, php_mysqli.dll, libmysql.dll

4 Open your php.ini file and find the line:

```
;extension=php_mysql.dll
```

Delete the semicolon to make the PHP engine load the MySQL module when it runs.

5 Beneath that, add this line:

```
extension=php_mysqli.dll
```

This loads the Improved MySQL module, which includes new functions available with versions of MySQL 4.1.3 and above.

You may need to restart the web server for these changes to take effect.

Improved MySQL and web hosting

This book assumes that by the time you read it, most people will be using PHP5 and MySQL 4.1.3 or higher. The following chapters will use PHP's Improved MySQL functions to work with the database, instead of the old functions (you can easily tell them apart: the old functions all start with mysql_ and the new ones use mysqli_).

At the time of writing, there were still quite a few web hosting companies who hadn't yet upgraded their servers to versions which support the mysqli functions. If you already have some web space which you plan to use for your PHP/MySQL work, check for mysqli compatibility with your hosting company.

If they don't support mysqli – and have no plans to upgrade any time soon – then you may want to consider moving to a more switched-on and future-proofed host! If for any reason this is not an option, you will need to download an older version of MySQL (4.0), and skip the mysqli bits in steps 3 and 5 of the PHP configuration tasks described above.

You may also need to refer to the PHP online manual or an older book than this, because some of the mysql functions work a little differently to the mysqli functions explained here.

9.3 Working with MySQL

This book is mainly concerned with PHP, and so most of the work we'll cover with regard to the MySQL database will be done using PHP. This means writing web pages which interact with a MySQL database, extracting data from it or writing data into it. However, it is a lot easier to work directly with MySQL to do the groundwork: creating a database, setting up the tables in it, etc.

To do this, you can either be a real tecchie and work from the MySQL command line, DOS-style, or you can take advantage of one of the MySQL client interfaces available. A GUI (Graphical User Interface) is easier to get started with if you have not used SQL before (SQL is the language used to talk to databases). However, you will need to learn SQL in any case in order to work with a database via PHP, so this is not a skill that can be skipped over for long!

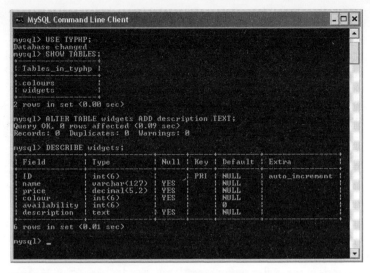

Working with MySQL from the command line

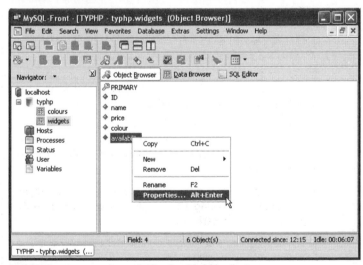

MySQL-Front, a popular and effective MySQL client.

The command line approach also has two advantages if you get stuck and need to ask for help on a web forum:

* It is universal – working from the command line is the same for all users, so any problems and solutions can be easily

shared. If your problem refers to a particular GUI, there will be a smaller pool of people in a position to help you out.

* It is the weapon of choice for the über-geeks who are most likely to be able to answer your question; they will respect a command-line user more and be more willing to answer your questions.

There is no shame in opting for a GUI – I may get shot for saying this, but they can actually be a lot nicer to work with than the command line. Even so, you should take the time to learn how to create and modify database tables using SQL. Any good GUI will offer the ability to use SQL statements directly, as well as its own menus and buttons.

But GUIs vary and cannot all be explained in any detail in this book, so roll up your sleeves and get ready to get your hands dirty in the black-and-white world of command line SQL ...

Summary

* The MySQL database can be freely downloaded from www.mysql.com.

* If you have a Windows PC, there is a version of MySQL which includes an installer program. This makes installing and configuring MySQL very simple.

* To get MySQL 4.1.3 and above working properly with PHP 5 and above, you need to download additional files from www.php.net, and change a couple of lines in the php.ini config file.

* MySQL databases can be administered via a DOS-style command line, or using a third-party client program with a graphical user interface.

* GUI clients are easier for beginners and often faster, but the command line approach has advantages when you need to ask for help from the online community.

10
introduction to SQL

In this chapter you will learn:

- what makes up a database
- what SQL is and why you need to know
- how to create a database and its tables using SQL
- how to put new data into the database
- how to retrieve and modify data

10.1 A brief overview of databases

A database is a storage house for information. Modern databases are 'relational', which means that instead of just chucking everything into one big pile, information is divided up into separate storage areas. These areas contain information which in some logical sense 'belongs' together, and they are linked (or 'related') to each other by cross-references.

For instance, in a typical shop database you might have one area to store customer contact details, and one to store product details. These are different kinds of information and it makes sense to keep them separate. You might then have a third area which stores sales information – records of which customers bought which products, when they bought them and how many they bought. Rather than repeating the contact and product details in every sales record, there are cross-references to the relevant customer and product records instead.

Database design

By far the most complicated thing about working with databases is getting the design right. There is a lot of theory around on relational databases, which is well worth a read if you want to learn how to build a good database. Unfortunately there's no room in this book for anything of the sort, so we'll just dive straight into building a simple database so that we can see how it works with PHP.

A little knowledge may sometimes be a dangerous thing, but in this case it'll get you quite a long way. If you use the basic instructions laid out here to build a database without referring to any further database theory, it will probably not be very efficient in database terms. Luckily, the difference between 'efficient' and 'inefficient' in database terms is pretty small until you start working with huge databases containing hundreds of thousands of pieces of information.

If you're reading this, you are probably not planning on overhauling a major corporate database next week, so we can safely assume that efficiency is not an overriding concern. Of course, the more you know, the better – if you are tempted to put this book down now and go and read up on relational databases theory, good on you. But if you're itching to get started and figure you can upgrade your skills later, that's fine too – we are good to go, and I'm a firm believer in learning through experience!

Tables, columns and records

As mentioned above, a database is a set of 'storage areas', which are properly called 'tables'. A table can be thought of as a grid: you have a fixed number of columns which determine the kind of data you're going to store in this table, and then an unlimited number of rows in which the actual data itself is stored. The rows in a table are called 'records'.

So in a table of customer details, for instance, you might have columns for first name, last name, telephone, address, etc. Each of your customers would be added as a separate record, with the relevant details being dropped into the appropriate columns. When you're designing a table, you need to think 'what bits of information do I want to store about this person/product/thing?' and make sure you have a column for each one. Columns come in several different types, depending on what kind of (and how much) data is to be stored in them.

Primary keys and indexing

One small piece of database design theory which you should know (because it's important *and* easy) is that any good table must have a primary key. This is a column which uniquely identifies a particular record, i.e. no two records can have the same value in the primary key column. Typically the primary key column is called something like 'ID' and is a number generated automatically by the database.

When you are looking for that record in future, if you specify its ID number, MySQL can quickly scan through the primary key column looking for that number. This is more reliable than looking for a customer called 'Joe Average', because there might be two such Joes. It is also much faster, because (a) computers understand numbers better (faster) than words, and (b), the primary key is an 'indexed field'.

This means that in addition to the record itself, the database maintains an index – a list of where exactly to find that record.

Other columns can also be indexed to speed up searches on the information in those columns (though as I said above, this doesn't really become a concern until you have a really massive database).

10.2 What is SQL?

Although the originator of SQL apparently refuses to say what it actually stands for, it is generally understood to mean Structured Query Language. SQL is the universal language of databases – whatever database you use, and whatever language you use to interact with it, you will always use SQL. In fact, every database has its own peculiarities and additional functions, but the same core commands are used whether you are interrogating an Oracle database via C#, or a MySQL database via PHP.

SQL syntax

SQL is easy really – there are just a few commands you need to know, and they all pretty much make instant sense to English speakers. You may have seen SQL code before – it looks something like this:

```
SELECT name, price FROM widgets WHERE
category='electronic';
```

Conventionally, the SQL command words are written in block capitals, so they are easily distinguished from the names of databases, tables and fields. In the example above, we are looking at a SELECT statement – one used to retrieve data from the database. We are asking the database to look in the widgets table and find us some name and price values. But we don't want all of them – just those records where the value in the category field is electronic.

All SQL statements end in a semicolon. Where values are specified they must be enclosed in single quotes if they are strings; numeric values can also be quoted, but do not have to be.

10.3 Creating a database with MySQL commands

Current versions of MySQL come with a command line client – open this from the Windows Start Menu, by choosing All Programs -> MySQL -> MySQL Server 4.1 -> MySQL Command Line Client. When the window opens you will be prompted to enter a password. This is the root user password you set when installing MySQL.

Type in the password and hit [Return]. You should see a screen like this:

Note that you can't use the mouse in the command line window – this is keyboard-only computing in an old-skool style!

Creating a database is very complicated, so pay attention to the following code, which you type at the mysql> prompt:

```
mysql> CREATE DATABASE database_name;
```

Got that? Hey, you're good! Yes, creating a database is really that easy – just CREATE DATABASE and then the name of your new database. Remember to end the line with a semicolon, and hit [Return] to execute the command.

Before you can perform any actions on a database, you need to tell the MySQL engine *which* database you want to use. Do this using the USE command:

```
mysql> USE database_name;
```

This will give you the message Database changed, which lets you know that you can now get to work on that database.

Naming databases and tables

Each element of a database has a name to identify it – the database itself, every table and column. To avoid confusion, these should not have spaces, and there are various naming conventions to handle this: some people use capital letters in the middle of the name (e.g. CustomerFirstName), others use underscores (customer_first_name). I prefer the second, as it seems easier to read, but you should do whatever you feel most comfortable with.

Choosing column types for tables

You now have a database, but it is just an empty shell – you need some tables in it. Let's start with a customers table, and draw up a plan of the information we want to store in it. We need to think of what kind of data is going in each column (text? numbers? both?) and establish what its maximum storage requirements are.

Column	Description/notes
id	ID field, primary key (integer, automatically generated); maximum number of customer records a few thousand.
first_name	Alphanumeric, max. a few dozen characters
last_name	Alphanumeric, max. a few dozen characters
tel	Telephone number (number, max. 20 digits)
fax	Fax number (number, max. 20 digits)
email	Alphanumeric, maximum a few dozen characters
address1	First line of address (alphanumeric, max. 100 or so characters)
address2	Second line of address (alphanumeric, max. 100 or so characters)
address3	Third line of address (alphanumeric, max. 100 or so characters)
address4	Fourth line of address (alphanumeric, max. 100 or so characters)

postcode	Alphanumeric, maximum 10 characters
notes	For keeping notes on customers – e.g. special requirements, etc. (alphanumeric, maximum a few thousand characters)
status	A code we can assign to customers to filter them in different ways: 1 = standard customers 2 = special customers with large repeat orders 3 = late payers – don't sell them too much on credit! etc.

Now we can decide what data type each column should be. It's worth tailoring the storage space available in each column to the maximum requirements, as it saves space and improves efficiency – but don't be too stingy. You want to make sure there's enough room for the largest piece of data you can think of, and then add in a little extra breathing space just in case.

For instance, we will probably only ever need the numbers 0 to a few thousand for our customer ID, so looking at the numeric column types below shows that a SMALLINT type would be ample. However, for the tiniest overhead of an extra 1 byte of storage space for each record, we could go for a MEDIUMINT and have up to 16 million customers. What the hell – no point starting a business if you're not going to be ambitious! Having said that, the upper limit of the BIGINT type is about 18 million trillion, so we probably don't need to go that far …

Numeric column types

Type	Storage limits	Bytes
TINYINT	–128 to 127 (or 0 to 255)	1
SMALLINT	–32,768 to 32,767 (or 0 to 65,535)	2
MEDIUMINT	–8,388,608 to 8,388,607 (or 0 to 16,777,215)	3
INT	–2,147,483,648 to 2,147,483,647 (or 0 to 4,294,967,295)	4

BIGINT	−9,223,372,036,854,775,808 to 9,223,372,036,854,775,807 (or 0 to 18,446,744,073,709,551,615)	8
DECIMAL(P,S)	Variable	P + 2

In the DECIMAL(P,S) type, P is the precision – how many digits – and S is the scale – the number of digits after the decimal point (e.g. DECIMAL(4,2) would allow a number of 99.99)

String column types

Type	Storage limits	Bytes
CHAR(N)	255 characters	N
VARCHAR(N)	N, where N is between 0 and 255	L + 1
TINYTEXT	255	L + 1
TEXT	65,535	L + 2
MEDIUMTEXT	16,777,216	L + 3
LONGTEXT	4,294,967,295	L + 4

L is the actual length of the string stored.

Date/time column types

Type	Storage format	Bytes
DATE	YYYY-MM-DD	3
DATETIME	YYYY-MM-DD HH:MM:SS	8
TIMESTAMP	NNNNNNNNNNNNNN (Unix time)	4
TIME	HH:MM:SS	3
YEAR	YYYY	1

A similar look at the storage requirements for the rest of our table would suggest we can safely use a VARCHAR type for most fields, except for notes, which should be TEXT, and status, which can be TINYINT. Note that we are treating the telephone and fax numbers as text strings rather than integers – this is so that leading zeroes are not ignored.

Creating the table using SQL

The syntax for an SQL statement to create a new table looks like this:

```
CREATE TABLE table_name (
column_1_name COLUMN 1 DEFINITION,
column_2_name COLUMN 2 DEFINITION);
```

The column definition can simply specify the type, but may also include constraints such as PRIMARY KEY. The definitions are enclosed in brackets, separated by commas. They are often written on a separate line to make the whole thing easier to read. If you are working from the command line, you can hit [Return] to move onto a new line: the commands are only executed when there is a semicolon marking the end of the statement.

So the SQL needed to create our customer data table looks like the listing below. Remember to select a database using 'USE' before trying to create the table!

```
mysql> CREATE TABLE customers (
    -> id MEDIUMINT UNSIGNED PRIMARY KEY
AUTO_INCREMENT,
    -> first_name VARCHAR(127),
    -> last_name VARCHAR(127) NOT NULL,
    -> tel VARCHAR(20),
    -> fax VARCHAR(20),
```

```
    -> email VARCHAR(127),
    -> address1 VARCHAR(127),
    -> address1 VARCHAR(127),
    -> address1 VARCHAR(127),
    -> address1 VARCHAR(127),
    -> postcode VARCHAR(10),
    -> notes TEXT,
    -> status TINYINT DEFAULT 1);
```

These definitions include some constraints we have not seen yet, which tighten the column definitions:

- UNSIGNED means that we don't need negative numbers – this gives us the integers from 0 to about 16 million instead of from minus 8m to plus 8m.

- PRIMARY KEY indicates that this column is the primary key for the table.

- AUTO_INCREMENT tells the database to insert a unique number for each record by adding 1 to the last record's number.

- NOT NULL means that this field must always contain some kind of value – it cannot be left blank – so in this case, every customer record must at least have a last name and telephone number (as well as an ID number).

- DEFAULT specifies a default value for the field – any record inserted which does not have a value explicitly set will take this one. In this case, we'll set the customer status to 1 by default, which is our code for a standard customer.

Altering tables

Before we move on to adding records to the table, let's just check that everything looks OK. Use the DESCRIBE command to list a table's columns and their definitions:

```
DESCRIBE customers;
```

If you spot a mistake, you can always alter the table structure using ALTER TABLE. With this, you need to specify the offending table and column, and what you want to do with it:

```
ALTER TABLE customers DROP fax;
```

(removes the fax column altogether)

DESCRIBE lists the table's columns and their definitions.

```
ADD birthday DATE AFTER notes;
```

(adds a new column after the notes column)

```
MODIFY tel VARCHAR(64);
```

(modifies the tel column definition)

```
CHANGE tel phone VARCHAR(32) AFTER fax;
```

(changes the tel column name and definition, and moves it to after the fax column)

And if you've really messed things up and you just want to ditch the whole lot and start again, there are always the drastic options:

```
DROP TABLE customers;
```

```
DROP DATABASE acme_widgets;
```

Just remember that if you DROP a table or database, you will lose any data stored in it, and there is no 'Undo' command – so use with caution!

10.4 Working with database records

When defining tables, there is no minimum or maximum number of records specified – we can do what we like with the data stored there, as long as it meets the constraints of the column definitions. We can add new records, pull one or more out for inspection, change the content of individual fields in existing records, or delete records completely.

Adding records to the database

The command used to add new records to a database is INSERT. You need to specify the table to insert data into, and the values for the fields. You don't need to give values for all the fields – you can leave some empty (NULL) or accept the default values.

```
mysql> INSERT INTO customers VALUES (
    -> DEFAULT, 'Miguel', 'de Cervantes', NULL,
NULL, NULL,
    -> 'Calle de la Imagen, 4', 'Alcala de
Henares', NULL,
    -> NULL, NULL, 'Haven\'t seen Miguel for
ages', DEFAULT);
```

Notice the backslash before the single apostrophe in 'Haven't' – as in PHP, this is an escape character to prevent MySQL interpreting it the wrong way.

In the example above, we have limited information and have to enter a load of NULLs to match the number of fields in the table (if you miss one out, you'll get an error). An alternative is to just specify the columns that we *do* have information for:

```
mysql> INSERT INTO customers (
    -> first_name, last_name, notes, address1,
address2)
    -> VALUES (
    -> 'Miguel', 'de Cervantes', 'Haven\'t seen
Miguel for ages',
    -> 'Calle de la Imagen, 4', 'Alcala de
Henares');
```

This has the added advantage that you don't have to remember which order the columns come in – as long as the bracketed values match up with the bracketed columns, it doesn't matter what order they are in the actual table.

Viewing records

To retrieve records from a database with SQL, you need to use a SELECT query. This is where I stick my head over the geek parapet and say that GUI clients are better than the command line. Try the following and you'll see what I mean ...

```
SELECT * FROM customers;
```

```
MySQL Command Line Client                                              - □ x
mysql> SELECT * FROM customers;

+----+------------+--------------+------+------+---------+-------------------+
| id | first_name | last_name    | tel  | fax  | email   | address1          |
 address2          | address3 | address4 | postcode | notes
   | status |
+----+------------+--------------+------+------+---------+-------------------+

| 1 | Miguel      | de Cervantes | NULL | NULL | NULL    | Calle de la Imagen, 4 |
Alcala de Henares | NULL     | NULL     | NULL     | Haven't seen Miguel for ag
es |      1 |

1 row in set (0.00 sec)

mysql> _
```

If you find this easy to read, insert a few more customer records
and then try this again. If you still find it a breeze to read, then
you are probably some kind of savant who doesn't need a database anyway, you can just keep it all in your head! A MySQL
client would show the data in a nice clear grid which you can
scroll through, instead of this forest of pipes and plus symbols.

Anyway, let's leave that aside for now – the purpose of this section is to explain the SQL, and the command line is still best for
that. Let's look at the query again: we specify the table to look in
with the word FROM, and the asterisk is a wildcard, meaning
'show me everything'. If we are only interested in certain fields,
we can tell MySQL to just show us those values, and not waste
time fetching all the other data:

    SELECT id, last_name, notes FROM customers;

```
MySQL Command Line Client                                              - □ x
2 rows in set (0.00 sec)

mysql> SELECT first_name, last_name, address1 FROM customers;
+------------+--------------+----------------------+
| first_name | last_name    | address1             |
+------------+--------------+----------------------+
| Miguel     | de Cervantes | Calle de la Imagen, 4 |
| William    | Shakespeare  | Bard's Lane          |
+------------+--------------+----------------------+
2 rows in set (0.00 sec)

mysql> SELECT id, last_name, notes FROM customers;
+----+--------------+------------------------------------------+
| id | last_name    | notes                                    |
+----+--------------+------------------------------------------+
| 1  | de Cervantes | Haven't seen Miguel for ages             |
| 2  | Shakespeare  | Must tell Bill about that play idea I had |
+----+--------------+------------------------------------------+
2 rows in set (0.00 sec)

mysql> _
```

Filtering records

Much of the time you will only be interested in a limited number of records, or just one at a time. In this case you need some way of filtering out the unwanted records and just returning the good stuff. This is done by adding a conditional expression to the SELECT query, using a WHERE clause.

```
SELECT first_name, last_name, FROM customers
WHERE id=2;
```

or

```
SELECT id, last_name, FROM customers WHERE
first_name='William';
```

```
MySQL Command Line Client                                    _ □ x
2 rows in set (0.00 sec)
mysql> SELECT id,last_name FROM customers WHERE first_name='William';
+----+-----------+
| id | last_name |
+----+-----------+
|  2 | Shakespeare |
+----+-----------+
1 row in set (0.00 sec)
mysql> SELECT first_name, last_name FROM customers WHERE id=2;
+------------+-----------+
| first_name | last_name |
+------------+-----------+
| William    | Shakespeare |
+------------+-----------+
1 row in set (0.00 sec)
mysql> _
```

The conditional expression does not have to be an exact match – you can use mathematical comparisons ...

```
SELECT name, price, FROM widgets WHERE id>10;
```

... or partial instead of exact string matches, using the LIKE operator, and % as a wildcard:

```
SELECT id FROM customers WHERE first_name LIKE
'Will%';
```

Modifying existing records

Suppose one of your customers moves house and you need to update their details with the new address. One (bad) way to approach this would be to just add a new record and remember to use that one instead of the old one when sending deliveries.

But after a few moves that will become confusing; or if your errandboy Granville takes the order, he might forget to use the new address. Besides, your order history will get all messed up.

A better solution would be to take the current record and just update it. We can do this in SQL using UPDATE and a WHERE clause to specify the record to update.

```
mysql> UPDATE customers SET
    -> address1='Globe Theatre', address2='London'
    -> WHERE id=2;
```

Unless you deliberately want to update more than one record at a time, you must ensure that the WHERE clause will only return the record you want to update. If you replaced the clause above with WHERE first_name='William', you could find that you've changed your address details for Messrs Clinton and Gates as well as Mr Shakespeare ...

Using MySQL to do the maths

When updating a record, you don't have to insert a fixed value – instead, you can get MySQL to look at the current value and do something to it. Suppose you have an additional column 'credit limit' in the customers table, and you're feeling generous, so you decide to increase everyone's limit by 10%. It would be very tedious to go through each record with a calculator, updating them one by one. Instead, you could do this:

```
UPDATE customers SET cr_lim = (cr_lim * 1.1);
```

This will go through the whole table (there is no WHERE clause to restrict the action to particular records), and multiply the current credit limit by 1.1 in each case.

Deleting records

If you've ever lived in a small apartment or house, you will probably have learned to be ruthless in disposing of junk you don't really need any more. Personally, I've found that the same habit filters through into my treatment of data, which is just plain wrong! Data storage space is not like a cramped understairs cupboard or attic, which soon gets cluttered up with old clothes and clapped-out printers. It is cheap and almost infinite, so before you delete anything, it's always worth thinking 'Will I really *never* want this information again?'

If there's even a shadow of a doubt, you might as well keep it. By including columns such as the 'status' column in your customers table, you can mark obsolete records as 'inactive'. Inactive records can be filtered out during your normal use of the database, so they don't clutter up your lists and reports, but if you ever *do* need to refer back to them, they're still safely stored.

Having said all that, there will still be times when a record can and should be deleted. In these cases, you need to use DELETE:

```
DELETE FROM customers WHERE id=1;
```

As with the DROP commands, use DELETE with care, because you can't un-delete a record you accidentally binned.

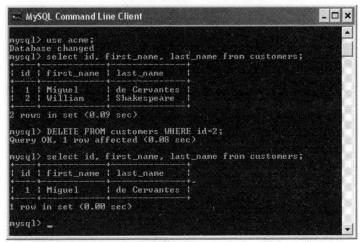

```
mysql> use acme;
Database changed
mysql> select id, first_name, last_name from customers;
+----+------------+-------------+
| id | first_name | last_name   |
+----+------------+-------------+
|  1 | Miguel     | de Cervantes |
|  2 | William    | Shakespeare  |
+----+------------+-------------+
2 rows in set (0.09 sec)

mysql> DELETE FROM customers WHERE id=2;
Query OK, 1 row affected (0.08 sec)

mysql> select id, first_name, last_name from customers;
+----+------------+-------------+
| id | first_name | last_name   |
+----+------------+-------------+
|  1 | Miguel     | de Cervantes |
+----+------------+-------------+
1 row in set (0.00 sec)

mysql>
```

Exercises

1 If you haven't already, create the 'acme' database and the 'customers' table in it, using the example given above as a guide. Now plan and add a new table called 'products' which stores details of the Acme Widget Company's products. Ensure that there are several columns of different types, including an id field, name, description, price, quantity available, operating instructions, and any others you want to include.

Hint: use the DECIMAL column type to format price values correctly.

2 Add some widgets to the products table.

3 Look up the name, ID and price of all widgets which:

(a) cost less than £9.99

(b) have something to do with screws (i.e. which include 'screw' in the product description. If you have not used that word in your descriptions, search for another one!)

4 The Acme January sale is on! Reduce the price of all widgets by 15% ('Hold it!' says the CEO – 'Not *all* the widgets, just the cheap ones! Don't reduce the price of any widgets worth more than £15.').

Summary

- A relational database is a data storage system consisting of discrete sets of data called tables, which are linked together via cross-references.

- Tables are defined by their columns, and data is stored in them as rows, or 'records'.

- Assess your data storage requirements carefully before setting up a database, and choose appropriate column types.

- SQL (Structured Query Language) is the language universally used to manage information in databases. It is not part of PHP, but is used alongside it.

- Use CREATE DATABASE... and CREATE TABLE... to create new databases and tables.

- Use ALTER TABLE... CHANGE/MODIFY/ADD/DROP... to alter the structure of a table.

- Use DROP DATABASE... and DROP TABLE... to permanently delete databases and tables.

- Use INSERT INTO... VALUES... to insert new records into the database.

- Use SELECT... FROM... WHERE... to retrieve data.

- Use UPDATE... SET... WHERE... to modify records.

- Use DELETE FROM... WHERE... to delete records.

using PHP with MySQL

In this chapter you will learn:

- how to use PHP to connect to a MySQL database
- how to use PHP to extract and display data from a database
- how to use PHP to add new records or work with existing ones

11.1 Connecting to MySQL from a PHP page

Remember those extra configuration fiddles we did back in Chapter 9 to get PHP working with MySQL? This is where they bear fruit. The mysqli module is a set of PHP functions designed for use with MySQL databases (recent versions). It includes functions for opening and closing connections to a database, executing queries, extracting information and putting it into arrays, plus a host of other specialized tasks which are way beyond what we need for the time being.

Opening and closing connections

Before a web page can talk to a database and swap information with it, you need to open a connection between them. To do this, you need four pieces of information:

- the host name of the database server
- a username
- a password
- the name of the database you want to work with.

You will need to get these from your ISP when you are dealing with a live site hosted on the Internet; but while you're working on your local machine, the host name is localhost and the username is root. If your password is 123 (it shouldn't be!) and you want to work on the acme database, you put all these into a 'connection string' like this:

```
$link =
mysqli_connect('localhost','root','123','acme');
```

This opens the connection and assigns it to the variable $link, which is needed by other functions, such as those used to execute queries. It is also needed to close the connection using the mysqli_close function:

```
mysqli_close($link);
```

Try putting this all into a page:

```
<HTML>
<BODY>
```

```
This page should open and then close a connec-
tion to a MySQL database. If there is a problem,
I'll get an error message here:
<?
$link =
mysqli_connect('localhost','root','123','acme');
mysqli_close($link);
?>
</BODY>
</HTML>
```

Since we're not doing anything with the connection, it's hard to see whether it's working or not! To test, try again with the wrong password:

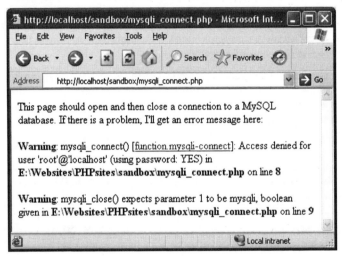

When to connect

A database can only have a certain number of connections open at any one time (the actual number will vary according to how the servers are set up). This means that it is very important to close any open connections as soon as possible once the web page has finished its business with the database.

However, in terms of speed and efficiency, opening a connection is generally the slowest part of any web page/database interaction. This means that it is not a good idea to open a connection immediately before every query to the database and close it again immediately afterwards. The optimum solution is to open a connection once per page, as late as possible (i.e. just before the very first query is made), and closed as soon as you are sure that it won't be needed again (i.e. after you have processed the results of the last query).

Don't hard-code the connection string!

Picture this: you've built a database-driven site so flashy it'll outshine Vegas itself. It's taken months of development work on your local machine to code up hundreds of pages, and finally it's time to transfer it to a live web server. Now you find ... that your ISP is (quite rightly) not going to let you have the root user password to their database server. And the web server is on a different machine from the database server, so the host name isn't 'localhost' any more. Every page which needs to connect to the database is now wrong and has to be amended. Gaah!

Or: you've put your connection string into a separate little file, and used `include_once()` to call it in the pages where you need it. Now you can move the site around as often as you like, and you only need to change one file each time ...

11.2 Extracting records from the database

OK, we know how to open a connection – how do we get PHP to execute SQL queries through it? The first step is to build the query and assign it to a variable:

```
$select = "SELECT first_name, last_name
FROM customers
    WHERE id=1";
```

The next step is to execute the query and assign the result to a variable. To do this we need the variables containing the connection string and the SQL query:

```
$result = mysqli_query($link, $select);
```

PHP now has the result of this query stashed away in a results object, referenced by `$result`. We can't just echo this onto the screen, because the results are not necessarily a simple string. A query might return hundreds of records, each one with many different fields and contents.

Displaying a single record

To get to the results of a query in a way that we can make use of, we need to separate out each field. The `mysqli_fetch_array()` function places the field names and values into an array so that we can reference each one individually:

```php
// assign the results to an array
$row = mysqli_fetch_array($result);

// get each array element and give it a variable
// name of its own
$fn = $row['first_name'];
$ln = $row['last_name'];

// print the results
echo <<<EOF
<h2>Query results:</h2>
First name: $fn <br/>
Last name: $ln <br/>
EOF;
```

Remember: all this must go *after* the connection string and before the line closing the connection!

Displaying multiple records

Instead of pulling out a specific record, suppose our query is designed to extract certain pieces of information from every record:

```
$select = "SELECT first_name, last_name
FROM customers";
```

This will probably yield more than one record in the result, so we have a problem: the array created by mysqli_fetch_array() only shows the values from the first record. To get at the values from the next record, we need to call mysqli_fetch_array() again. And again for the next record, and the next! We could type it out again each time, but besides being longwinded, we would need to know in advance how many records the query is going to return.

Instead, we can just loop through the result object, putting each record into a fresh array, pulling the values out of it and displaying them.

```
// as long as there is a record, keep looping
while ($row = mysqli_fetch_array($result)) {
// get each element and put it in a variable
   $fn = $row['first_name'];
   $ln = $row['last_name'];
   // print them out
   echo "Name: $fn $ln <br/> <br/>";
// loop back to the next record
}
```

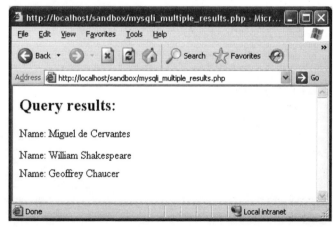

Displaying records in a table

If you are displaying several fields from each record, and there might be many records in the result, it is often useful to tabulate your results for easier reading. The first row containing the column headings can be put in your page as normal HTML, and you use the while loop to write each record into the table as a new row. Finally, the closing table tags can be added as normal HTML again.

```
<!--set up the table -->
<TABLE BORDER="1" CELLPADDING="5">
 <TR>
   <TH>First name</TH>
   <TH>Last name</TH>
   <TH>Telephone</TH>
   <TH>Email address</TH>
 </TR>
<?
// build and execute the query
$select = "SELECT first_name, last_name, tel, email
FROM customers";
$result = mysqli_query($link, $select);

// loop through the results
while ($row = mysqli_fetch_array($result)) {
// get each element and put it in a variable
$fn = $row['first_name'];
$ln = $row['last_name'];

   // print out the code for each row
   echo <<<END
 <TR>
   <TD>$fn</TD>
   <TD>$ln</TD>
   <TD>$tel</TD>
   <TD>$email</TD>
 </TR>
END;
}
?>
<!-- Close table -->
</TABLE>
```

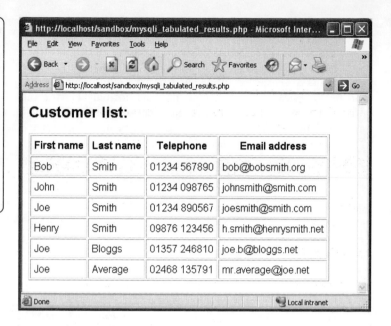

Sorting records

In the last chapter we learned how to filter out records matching certain criteria using a WHERE clause in the SELECT statement. There is another very handy clause we can add to produce a more useful set of results: the ORDER BY clause. As you might expect, this tells the database to take all the records which match your SELECT criteria, and sort them into a particular order.

Sorting is alphabetical and/or numeric, and is in ascending order by default (i.e. A to Z and lowest number to highest number). So for instance, to sort our customer list into alphabetical order of surname, we would amend the query to look like this:

```
$select = "SELECT first_name, last_name,tel, email
    FROM customers
    ORDER BY last_name";
```

If you have a lot of similar surnames in your customer list, you might want to sort on first name as well. The ORDER BY clause allows you to sort on as many columns as you like – just list them in the order of their sorting priority, separated by commas:

```
$select = "SELECT first_name, last_name, tel, email
    FROM customers
    ORDER BY last_name, first_name";
```

Or if you are very friendly with most of your customers and find it easier to work with first names first:

```
$select = "SELECT first_name, last_name, tel, email
    FROM customers
    ORDER BY first_name, last_name";
```

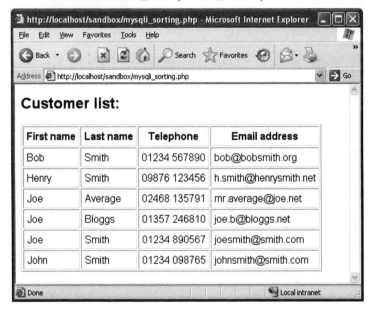

Filtering records

Using the SQL WHERE clause is by far the best way to narrow down a database search – there is no point getting the database server to send hundreds of records to the web server and then using conditional expressions in PHP to filter a few of them out to display on a web page. Your queries should always return just as many results as you want to use, and no more. But there are times when some post-database processing is useful, perhaps to single out certain records for special treatment.

For instance, we might want to highlight certain customers according to the status we have given them. To do this we will need

to supply some CSS styles, and a conditional expression inside
the loop which fetches and displays the query results:

```
<STYLE>
.normal {background-color: #FFFFFF; color:
#000000;}
.green {background-color: #00FF00; color:
#000000;}
.red {background-color: #FF0000; color:
#FFFFFF;}
</STYLE>

<?
while ($row = mysqli_fetch_array($result)) {
   $fn = $row['first_name'];
   $ln = $row['last_name'];
   $tel = $row['tel'];
   $email = $row['email'];
   $status = $row['status'];

   // determine row class by status
   if ($status==2) {
      $row_class = "green";
   } elseif ($status==3) {
      $row_class = "red";
   } else {
      $row_class = "normal";
   }

   echo <<<END
 <TR class="$row_class">
   <TD>$fn</TD>
   <TD>$ln</TD>
   <TD>$tel</TD>
   <TD>$email</TD>
 </TR>
END;
}
?>
```

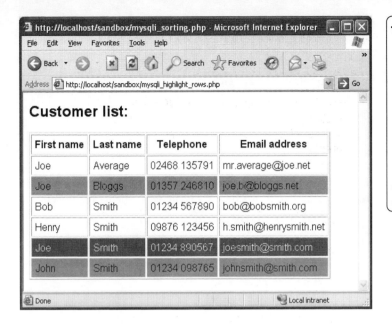

11.3 Putting data into the database

To get information into a database from a web page, we obviously need a form to receive the user inputs, and we also need a script to handle that form and its data. The script will gather up the data from the form inputs (and do any validation if required). If the data meets the validation criteria, the script will put the data into the database using an INSERT or UPDATE query. Finally, it should check that the insertion or update went smoothly, and confirm the success or warn if anything went awry.

Inserting a new record

We looked at handling and validating form data in Chapter 7, so I won't go over it in detail again here. Also, to avoid cluttering up the page with unnecessary code, I'll keep the validation to a minimum. The main thing to note is that when an INSERT or UPDATE query is executed, there is no result object to be returned. Instead, PHP returns TRUE if the query was executed successfully or FALSE if not. We can use this to pass an appropriate message to the user:

```
$insert = "INSERT INTO customers
   (first_name, last_name)
   VALUES ('$fn', '$ln')";

// execute query and check for success
if (!mysqli_query($link, $insert)) {
   $msg = "Error inserting data";
} else {
   $msg = "Record successfully added";
}
```

Here is a full code listing for a simple INSERT form for the *Customers* table (we'll just deal with the name fields for now):

```
<h2>Add new Customer</h2>
<STYLE>
.error {padding: 10px; color: #CC0000; font-
weight: bold;}
</STYLE>

<?
// has form been submitted?
if ($_POST) {
   // create empty error variable
   $msg = "";

   // put form data into variable variables
   foreach($_POST as $k => $v) {
      $v = trim($v) ;
      $$k = $v ;

      // check for data in both fields
      if ($v=="") {
         $msg = "Please fill in both fields";
      }
   }

   // if all data is there, build query
   if ($msg=="") {
      $insert = "INSERT INTO customers
         (first_name, last_name)
         VALUES ('$fn', '$ln')";
```

```php
        // open db connection
        include 'includes/db_conn.txt';

        // execute query and check for success
        if (!mysqli_query($link, $insert)) {
           $msg = "Error inserting data";
        } else {
           $msg = "Record successfully added";
           // set vars to "" for next form input
           $fn = $ln = "";
        }
        mysqli_close($link);
    }

    // print error or success messages
    echo "<div class=\"error\">$msg</div>";

// if not submitted, create blank vars for form
inputs
} else {
    $fn = $ln = "";
}
?>

<FORM METHOD="post" ACTION="<? echo
$_SERVER['PHP_SELF'] ?>">
<TABLE BORDER="1" CELLPADDING="5">
 <TR>
   <TH>First name</TH>
   <TH>Last name</TH>
 </TR>
 <TR>
   <TD><INPUT TYPE="text" NAME="fn" VALUE="<?
echo $fn ?>" /></TD>
   <TD><INPUT TYPE="text" NAME="ln" VALUE="<?
echo $ln ?>" /></TD>
 </TR>
</TABLE>
<BR/>
<INPUT TYPE="submit" VALUE="Add to database" />
<INPUT TYPE="reset" VALUE="Cancel" />
</FORM>
```

Updating an existing record

This process is handled in much the same way as inserting a new record, except that this time, our first task is to specify and locate the record to be updated. Let's add an extra column to our customer list, which contains 'Edit details' links. This will specify the customer's ID number, because we know that it is unique in the database. The update query should affect exactly *one* record, and no more:

```php
while ($row = mysqli_fetch_array($result)) {
    $fn = $row['first_name'];
    $ln = $row['last_name'];
    $id = $row['Id'];

    echo <<<END
  <TR>
    <TD>$fn</TD>
    <TD>$ln</TD>
    <TD><a href="editcust.php?id=$id">Edit de-
tails</a></TD>
  </TR>
END;
}
```

Altering the database structure via the web

You can use web forms to alter or create tables (or even whole new databases), using the same query format as for inserting into or updating tables. But unless your site requires the regular creation of many tables, creating the necessary interface is probably more trouble than it's worth!

Our next script, editcust.php, will need to pick up the customer ID number from the query string, and then use it to locate the relevant record in the database. The full code will be listed in a few pages, but let's cannibalize a few extracts from it first so that we can see what's going on. To start with, a user comes to this page via the link, so we need to get the ID and look it up in the database:

```
$id = $_GET['id'];
$select = "SELECT * FROM customers WHERE
Id=$id";
$result = mysqli_query($link, $select);
```

Now we need to check that there really is a matching record in the database. To do this we make use of another PHP/MySQL function, mysqli_num_rows(). This function takes the result object as its argument, and returns the number of records which it contains. If there are zero results, no matches were found, and we need an error message.

```
if (mysqli_num_rows($result) < 1) {
    $msg = "No customer with that ID found!";
```

If the record is found, then we need to get the current data out and display it in a form:

```
} else {
    // assign the results to an array
    while ($row = mysqli_fetch_array($result)) {
        $fn = $row['first_name'];
        $ln = $row['last_name'];
        $tel = $row['tel'];
        $email = $row['email'];

        // produce code for this row
        $table_row = <<<END
```

```
  <TR>
    <TD><INPUT TYPE="text" NAME="fn" VALUE="$fn" /
></TD>
    <TD><INPUT TYPE="text" NAME="ln" VALUE="$ln" /
></TD>
    <TD><INPUT TYPE="text" NAME="tel" VALUE="$tel"
/></TD>
    <TD><INPUT TYPE="text" NAME="email"
VALUE="$email" /></TD>
  </TR>
END;
    }
}
```

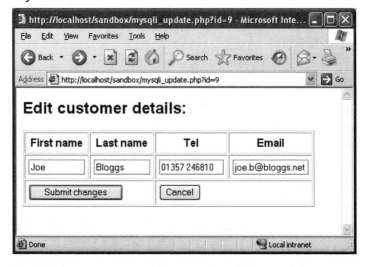

Keeping code and content apart

As you may have decided for yourself while working through some of these later examples, a script can quickly become quite hard to follow on the page, especially if we keep breaking out of PHP and into HTML. It is good practice to keep the static and dynamic parts of the page as separate as possible.

For instance in the current example, instead of typing the static HTML code for the table header into the middle of our PHP logic, we've assigned the HTML code for the table row to a PHP variable. Then, once we've finished all our processing, we can switch over to HTML to build the static parts of the page display, pulling in the variable for the dynamic row. This will make debugging much easier later on. (Have I already mentioned that you should leave copious 'notes to self' in your code? It's easy to assume you know what's going on, but when you come back to a script a few months after writing it, you will have forgotten why on earth you put that **foreach** loop in there!)

Now we have located the record to be updated, and we have a form to edit the data ... which goes nowhere at the moment. We need to add some form handling, so that if the page contains **$_POST** data, we can take the results of the form and put them into the **UPDATE** query. The MySQL part of this process will look like this:

```
// build query from form data
$update = "UPDATE customers SET
        first_name='$fn', last_name='$ln',
        tel='$tel', email='$email'
        WHERE Id=$id";

// execute query and check for success
if (!mysqli_query($link, $update)) {
   $msg = "Error updating data";
} else {
   $msg = "Record successfully updated.";
}
```

As with the **INSERT** query, there is no result set generated by executing an **UPDATE** query, so we just run a quick Boolean check on whether or not it was executed successfully, and give appropriate feedback to the user.

Full code listing

To see how all those pieces link together, here's the full code listing for the page which edits customer details:

```
<HTML>
<HEAD>
<STYLE>
BODY {font-family:arial;}
.error {font-weight:bold; color:#FF0000;}
</STYLE>
```

```
</HEAD>
<BODY>
<h2>Edit customer details:</h2>
<?

// connect to the database
include 'includes/db_conn.txt';

// has the form been submitted?
if ($_POST) {
   foreach($_POST as $k => $v) {
      $v = trim($v) ;
      $$k = $v;
   }

   // build UPDATE query
   $update = "UPDATE customers SET
      first_name='$fn', last_name='$ln',
      tel='$tel', email='$email'
      WHERE Id=$id";

   // execute query and check for success
   if (!mysqli_query($link, $update)) {
      $msg = "Error updating data";
   } else {
      $msg = "Record successfully updated:";

      // write table row confirming data
      $table_row = <<<EOR
      <TR>
         <TD>$fn</TD>
         <TD>$ln</TD>
         <TD>$tel</TD>
         <TD>$email</TD>
      </TR>
      EOR;
   }

// if not posted, check that an Id has been
//passed via the URL
} else {
```

```php
if (!IsSet($_GET['id'])) {
   $msg = "No customer selected!";
} else {
   $id = $_GET['id'];

   // build and execute the query
   $select = "SELECT first_name, last_name,
     tel, email FROM customers WHERE Id=$id";
   $result = mysqli_query($link, $select);

   // check that the record exists
   if (mysqli_num_rows($result)<1) {
     $msg = "No customer with that ID found!";
   } else {
   // set vars for form code
   $form_start = "<FORM METHOD=\"post\"ACTION=
     \"" . $_SERVER['PHP_SELF'] . "\">";
     $form_end = <<<EOF
     <TR>
        <TD COLSPAN="2"><INPUT TYPE="submit"
           VALUE="Submit changes" /></TD>
        <TD COLSPAN="2"><INPUT TYPE="reset"
           VALUE="Cancel" /></TD>
     </TR>
     </FORM>
     EOF;

// assign the results to an array
while ($row = mysqli_fetch_array($result)) {
   $fn = $row['first_name'];
   $ln = $row['last_name'];
   $tel = $row['tel'];
   $email = $row['email'];

   // write table row with form fields
   $table_row = <<<EOR
 <TR>
   <TD><INPUT TYPE="text" NAME="fn"
     VALUE="$fn" SIZE="10"/></TD>
   <TD><INPUT TYPE="text" NAME="ln"
     VALUE="$ln" SIZE="10"/></TD>
```

```
            <TD><INPUT TYPE="text" NAME="tel"
               VALUE="$tel" SIZE="12"/></TD>
            <TD><INPUT TYPE="text" NAME="email"
               VALUE="$email" SIZE="15"/></TD>
            </TR>
            EOR;
        }
        // end 'if record exists' if
        }
    // end 'if ID given in URL' if
    }
// end 'if form posted' if
}

// close connection
mysqli_close($link);

//print error/success message
echo (IsSet($msg)) ? "<div
class=\"error\">$msg</div>" : "";
?>

<TABLE BORDER="1" CELLPADDING="5">
<!-- Show start-of-form code if form needed -->
<? echo (IsSet($form_start)) ? $form_start : "";
?>
<INPUT TYPE="HIDDEN" NAME="id" VALUE="<? echo
$id ?>" />
 <TR>
   <TH>First name</TH>
   <TH>Last name</TH>
   <TH>Tel</TH>
   <TH>Email</TH>
 </TR>
<!-- Show appropriate table row code (none set
if there were errors) -->
<? echo (IsSet($table_row)) ? $table_row : "";
?>

<!-- Show end-of-form code if we are displaying
the form -->
```

```
<? echo (IsSet($form_end)) ? $form_end : ""; ?>
</TABLE>

<br/><a href="custlist.php">Back to customer
list</a>
</BODY>
</HTML>
```

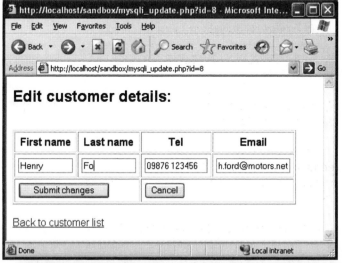

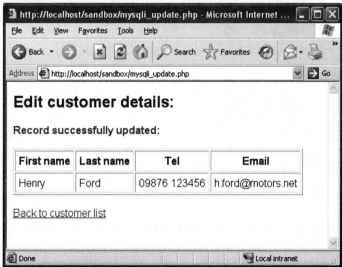

Exercises

1 Take the code listings given in this chapter and expand them so that they include all fields in the Acme customers table. You should end up with a suite of scripts to list and edit existing customers, or add new ones.

2 Write scripts to do the same for Acme's products.

3 Write a script which allows Acme's sales managers to adjust prices by a percentage across all products.

Summary

- PHP uses special MySQL functions to pass SQL queries to a MySQL database.

- `mysqli_connect()` will open a connection to a database.

- You can write out SQL queries as a string and assign them to variables, then use `mysqli_query()` to execute them.

- When executed, INSERT queries return all their results folded into one results object.

- `mysqli_fetch_array()` can parse this object into an array so that you can access the results as separate PHP variables.

- To display multiple records, loop through this array, processing the relevant data on each pass.

- INSERT and UPDATE queries can also be executed using `mysqli_query()`, but they give no result object.

12

converting ASP to PHP

In this chapter you will learn:

- how to use a popular free tool to convert ASP to PHP

- pitfalls to watch out for when doing a conversion

12.1 Why change all my old code?

If you're reading this, you have probably already decided that PHP is a better choice than ASP, so the simple answer is 'because it's better'. You are probably also aware that the old kind of ASP is on its way out and will need to be replaced at some point anyway – whether it's by PHP or by continuing down the Microsoft path to .NET.

Having said that, going through a whole site (even if it's not some huge database-driven megalith) is a fair chunk of work. It's going to be tempting to leave the old ASP code there and just hack it about when you need to. And if the site is ticking over nicely as it is and won't need any significant development in the near future, this might be the best thing to do. The same applies if you know that it's about time for a major overhaul anyway – no point in converting something which is going to be trashed and rebuilt from scratch in a couple of months' time.

But if you are updating and adding to the site fairly regularly, if it's a growing site which you expect to be working on in a year, two years' time, then you want to grit your teeth and get it done now. Every time you put off the conversion and add some new pages or functionality using ASP instead, you're just making the job bigger when it finally does come.

Translate or rebuild?

Of course, the main thing that makes conversion unappealing is that it's going to be a fiddly, boring job. You're going to have to comb through all those pages replacing <%s with <?s, swapping `switch` structures for `select`s, curly braces for `then`s, etcetera. No interesting new development issues to think through, just drudgery. You can imagine your eyes swelling up from all the staring at the screen, your fingers cramping with RSI, and your brain seizing up from the boredom. No fun.

Actually, it doesn't have to be like that. It's often worth taking the opportunity to reorganize the structure of the page, rather than just translating the old code into PHP. If your sites and/or clients are anything like mine, then over time the page functions will have come to bear very little resemblance to the original requirements. If these shifts happen little by little, to tight deadlines and budgets (sound familiar?), then the code logic is probably not as tight as it could be. If you get the chance, I'd consider a proper rebuild. (I know, your conversion project is also subject to tight deadlines and tight budgets! But it's worth pushing for if possible.)

However, even if you end up restructuring quite radically, there are still whole chunks of logic which remain more or less intact, and you will have to either convert these from ASP to PHP, or rewrite them from scratch. Luckily, there are tools available to ease the pain of the tedious conversion tasks, leaving you free to concentrate on the more interesting bits.

12.2 About ASP2PHP

ASP2PHP is a freeware tool which you can download and use to help you convert legacy ASP code into PHP. It is basically a rocket-powered search and replace routine which hunts through the text of your old web pages, replacing anything it recognizes as ASP with some nice new PHP. It works mainly with VBScript, the most common ASP scripting language, but claims to handle some JScript as well.

It's not foolproof of course, and you will almost certainly need to go through by hand to finish the job off. But it does take care of all the routine conversion chores, and actually handles the complex stuff very well too. Whether you are planning to just translate from ASP to PHP or taking the opportunity to restructure, a quick whip-through with this tool is a great time-saver.

Supporting free software

It sounds kind of daft to say 'support free software by paying for it', but you know what I mean. Freeware would still exist even if nobody ever clicked the PayPal donate buttons on the download sites, but if someone gives me something useful or valuable, shouldn't I give something back? If I'm going to save time and effort by using the fruits of someone else's labour, it seems only fair to pay them back somehow.

The easiest way is to send a small payment and a thank you note via whatever payment system they use (ASP2PHP uses PayPal). If you're not in a position to do this, or you would rather return a favour for a favour instead of using cold cash, think of something you can do for the developer(s). At the very least, you should acknowledge the help you've had by providing a credit and link somewhere on your converted site.

Downloading the tool

The software is available for Unix and Windows platforms at http://asp2php.naken.cc/download.php. The Unix versions need to be installed from the command line, but the Windows version is a single executable file – just extract it from the ZIP file and stash it somewhere on your hard drive.

To check that it's there and working, open a DOS prompt window (from the **Start** menu, use **All Programs -> Accessories -> Command Prompt**).

Now go to the directory where you saved *asp2php.exe*. If your DOS is a little rusty (or non-existent), you need to use the change directory command cd. Type cd\ to go back to the root of that drive; cd.. (two dots) to go back up one level; and cd directoryname to go to a directory at the current level.

Now type `asp2php.exe` at the command prompt: if all is well you should see a list of the command line options – a sort of mini help file.

ASP2PHP GUIs

For those of you with an aversion to command line work, there are some GUIs available. Mike Kohn, the developer who wrote ASP2PHP, has a list of them on his website at http://asp2php.naken.cc. I have to say though, I've had more success with the command line version – it isn't hard to get the hang of it!

12.3 Using ASP2PHP

First of all, make a plan: when the program does the conversion, it will want to know where to save the newly-created PHP files. You may want to build a directory structure in parallel to the old ASP one, or you might be happy to just drop the PHP files into the same directories as their ASP counterparts. The extensions will be different so there's no danger of getting them muddled up.

Whatever you decide to do, just remember that the conversion will not change any directory names or links inside your pages, except to change the .asp extension to .php. For instance, a link to /tools/customer/edit.asp would become /tools/cus-tomer/edit.php, even if you decided for some reason to save the PHP version of edit.asp in a directory called 'punter' instead of 'customer'. This means you have to manually edit any links affected by the change of directory name or structure.

Syntax

There is only one command to ASP2PHP, asp2php. This is followed by a number of options, of which only one is required (the destination file or directory). At the end of the line, the source file or directory is given. So at its most basic, the syntax is this:

```
>asp2php -o output.php input.asp
```

This looks up the original ASP file *input.asp*, and saves the PHP conversion as *output.php*. The –o flag stands for 'output'.

Set path

In the example above, we're assuming that the input and output files are all in the same directory as *asp2php.exe*. Normally that will not be the case: you would find your way to the directories where the input files are, and then set the DOS path to where the .exe file lives. For instance:

```
C:\Documents and Settings\Nat>
C:\Documents and Settings\Nat> E:
E:\> cd Websites\Acme
E:\Websites\Acme> set path=C:\PHP\asp2php
E:\Websites\Acme> asp2php -o customers.php
customers.asp
```

If you don't set the path, then you have to type in the full path to the .exe file each time you call it:

```
E:\Websites\Acme> C:\PHP\asp2php\asp2php -o
customers.php customers.asp
```

Optional flags

At the time of writing, the current version of ASP2PHP has 23 optional extra flags for specifying how to handle different aspects of the conversion. Here are some of the more useful:

-o   specifies output file/directory, e.g.

```
-o myfile.php (file)
```

```
-o dirs\mydir (directory)
```

-dir   input and output are directories – used to process multiple files

-mysql   convert database functions to MySQL

-includes   changes ASP #include to PHP's require()

-addextension   when processing a whole directory of files, ASP2PHP will look for files ending in .asp, .asa and .aspx by default. If you have includes ending in other extensions such as .txt or .inc, use this flag to specify them. You need to set each extension with a separate instance of the flag. e.g.

```
-addextension .txt -addextension .inc
```

-global_asa   If your ASP files used a *global.asa* file, set this flag to include *global.php* in all pages.

-change_response_links   Any links ending in .asp which appear in Response.Write statements in the ASP code will be changed to .php.

You can review the full list of options by typing asp2php at the command line.

I would recommend that you routinely include the -includes and -change_response_links flags for all conversions. They don't do any harm if there is nothing to convert, and they save you time if there is!

Converting whole directories

Since the whole point of using this tool is to save time and effort, we really need to look at converting lots of files at once. This is done with the -dir flag, which tells the program to go through the specified directory and convert any ASP files it finds there. In this case, the input and output are directory names rather than individual filenames:

```
asp2php -o php\products -dir products
```

When converting directories containing included files, you may need to set the -addextension flag so that files with extensions other than .asp are also converted:

```
asp2php -addextension .txt -addextension .inc -o
php\products -dir products
```

Any files which are not flagged up for conversion are copied across to the new directory – so you can convert your ASP files and copy across any images and documents in one go.

12.4 Some gotchas and 'what the ...?'s

ASP2PHP is a very useful little tool for taking the donkey work out of a conversion job. It is however, a free tool provided by the sheer goodwill of a generous developer, not a destruction-tested commercial product, and there are a few weird things to watch out for. Some or all of the issues below may have been fixed by the time you read this, or there may be new ones, but it's worth noting these anyway.

Empty files

Don't try to set the input and output filenames the same, or you can end up with an empty file. If you want the PHP file to have the same name as when it was an ASP file (as you might if it was an included file ending in .txt), you should give it a different name or a .php extension and then change it later manually.

Rogue directories

If you convert a directory without creating the destination directory first (using something like Windows Explorer), ASP2PHP will create the directory for you and then put the files in it. But it also seems to create an extra directory called '-p' for no particular reason. There's nothing in it, and you can just delete it afterwards. Or create the directory before doing the conversion.

File extensions on directory conversions

If you convert an individual file, you can give it whatever file extension you like. If you want the PHP conversion of header.txt to be called header.inc, or even header.bob, you can do so:

```
asp2php -o php\header.bob header.txt
```

But when converting a whole directory, all filenames are given a .php extension. This is usually fine, because you want most of your files to have that extension. But if you have a load of included files in your ASP pages which have .txt or .inc extensions, it is not very useful to have them renamed to .php. This is because the paths and filenames written into other pages will remain the same even after conversion. An ASP page which calls an included file with this line:

```
<!- #include file="ssi/header.txt" ->
```

Will become a PHP file which features this line:

```
<?php require("ssi/header.txt"); ?>
```

But unfortunately, since you converted all the included files in one batch, header.txt is now called header.php.

There's not a lot you can do about this, except be aware of it, and go and change the extensions back manually where necessary.

ADODB objects and properties

ASP2PHP has problems with converting some of the code used to set properties of ADODB objects. Suppose for instance you have a RecordSet object and you try to set its properties like this:

```
Set MyRS.ActiveConnection=conn
```

The ASP2PHP parser reads the keyword Set and expects a simple var=value expression to follow. So when it encounters a full stop instead of an equals sign, it gets confused; the conversion continues but this bit is converted wrongly.

MySQL(i)

At the time of writing, ASP2PHP handles MySQL database interactions using the old `mysql_` functions, not `mysqli_`. No doubt there will be an upgrade with a `mysqli_` option, but for now (unless you're building for a pre-MySQL 4.3.1 environment), you will have to go through and tweak the database sections.

Read the error report!

After running a conversion, scroll back up through the command line window to check for errors reported during the process. When the parser comes across anything it has trouble with, it will throw an error. These are generally quite informative notes, and come with a line reference to the original ASP file, so you can look up the problem and address it before you try any testing.

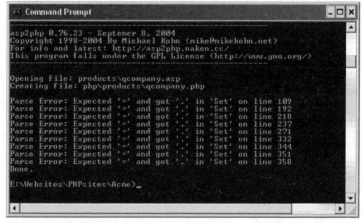

Summary

* If you have a site written in ASP/VBScript, now is a good time to think about converting it to PHP.

* You can use a freeware tool such as ASP2PHP to carry out the bulk of the conversion job.

* After converting you can run through and tidy up the odd bits that got lost in translation, or take the opportunity to restructure your logic to better suit current and anticipated future needs.

13

section

reference

In this chapter you will find:

- a summary of common variables predefined in PHP
- a summary of common PHP operators and functions
- a summary of common SQL commands
- links to further resources on the Internet

13.1 Predefined variables

These are some of the more common variables predefined in PHP, which can be accessed by a script at any time via the appropriate superglobal array, e.g.:

```
echo "This script is located at: " .
$_SERVER['PHP_SELF']
```

$_SERVER variables

Most $_SERVER variables provide information about the server that the script is running on, which is of limited use to most users.

There are however a couple of handy variables such as PHP_SELF which can be used to make your code more portable. There are also some which pick up information about the end user's browser and operating system from the HTTP headers, which can be useful for tailoring information to their needs.

HTTP_ACCEPT_LANGUAGE   Language settings on the user's browser, in code form – e.g. en-gb for UK English, fr for French, es-mx for Mexican Spanish.

HTTP_REFERER   If the user arrived at this page by following a link from another page, this gives the URL of that page.

HTTP_USER_AGENT   The user's browser and operating system details.

PHP_SELF   The path to the script currently running, starting at the server's web root (e.g. /mydir/myfile.php).

QUERY_STRING   The query string (if any) appended to the current URL.

SCRIPT_FILENAME   The full server path to the current script, including the disk drive letter (e.g. E:\web\mydir\myfile.php).

SERVER_NAME   The server your script is running on.

Other superglobal arrays

The contents of these arrays are not predefined and will vary according to what your script has added to them, along with any user input.

$_COOKIE   Contains variables stored on the current user's machine in cookies issued by the current server.

$_GET   Contains variables stored from a previous page via the GET method (i.e. in the URL query string).

$_POST   Contains variables stored from a previous page via the POST method (i.e. via submitted forms).

$_REQUEST   This is a kind of super-superglobal, which contains all the variables contained in the $_GET, $_POST, and $_COOKIE superglobals.

$_SESSION   Contains variables stored as part of the current user's session.

13.2 Some common PHP operators

Operators are symbols which have special meanings to the PHP parser. They include familiar mathematical operators such as + and –, as well as 'comparison operators' which are used to compare one value with another, and 'assignment operators' which assign values to variables.

String and assignment operators

.   Concatenates two strings, e.g.

```
"Hel" . "lo" // returns "Hello"
```

.=   Concatenates the string on the right to the current value of the variable on the left, e.g.

```
$txt = "Hel" // $txt .= "lo" // $txt is now "Hello"
```

=   Assigns the value on the right to the variable on the left, e.g.

```
$txt="Hello" // $txt is now "Hello"
```

=>   Defines the key and value of an array element, e.g.

```
$array = ("key_A" => "value_1", "key_B" =>
"value_2")
```

Mathematical operators

Standard operators: plus (+), minus(-), divide(/), multiply(*)

+= Adds the number on the right to the current value of the variable on the left, e.g.

```
$n = 5
$n += 6 // $n is now 11
```

-= Subtracts the number on the right from the current value of the variable on the left, e.g.

```
$n = 11
$n -= 6 // $n is now 5
```

/= Divides the current value of the variable on the left by the number on the right, e.g.

```
$n = 12
$n /= 3 // $n is now 4
```

*= Multiplies the current value of the variable on the left by the number on the right, e.g.

```
$n = 2
$n *= 4 //$n is now 8
```

Comparison operators

<   Is the number on the left less than the number on the right?

>   Is the number on the left greater than the number on the right?

<= Is the number on the left less than or equal to the number on the right?

>= Is the number on the left greater than or equal to the number on the right?

== Is the number or string on the left equal to the number or string on the right?

=== As above, and are they also of the same type? This is different to the == operator above, because it will distinguish between a zero and the Boolean value FALSE.

!= Is the number or string on the left different to the number or string on the right?

!== As above, but distinguishes between items of the same value but different types.

&& The AND operator, used to combine two different conditions into one (both conditions have to be TRUE for the overall result to be TRUE).

|| The OR operator, used to combine two different conditions into one (if either condition is TRUE, then the overall result is TRUE).

13.3 Some common PHP functions

This reference list only covers the functions used in this book (plus a few extras), and is intended as a reminder rather than a full set of instructions. For more details, use the index to look up the relevant section of the book. Or for a full breakdown of how to use any PHP function and all its arguments, refer to the PHP manual at http://www.php.net/manual/en.

Output and script functions

echo 'text'   Sends the string enclosed in quotes as part of the output to the browser.

echo "text and $str"   As above, except using double quotes means that any variables encountered in the string to be displayed will be parsed (i.e. their contents used instead of literally outputting a dollar sign and the variable name).

include path   Takes the contents of the file specified by path and parses it as if it were written into the current script.

include_once path   As above, but will prevent the inclusion of the same file (specified by path) twice. Useful when including snippets of code which would generate fatal errors if they were repeated (e.g. functions, which must not be redefined).

require path   Works in the same way as include, but if the included file is not found, a fatal error will be generated rather than just a warning – i.e. the script will stop and the page will stop loading.

print   Synonym of echo. There are minor technical differences, but in practice they are as good as identical functions.

return Assigns the output of a function. E.g. you have a function mashup($x) which processes $x in some way so as to give $y. Adding the line **return** $y to the end of the function means that mashup($x) has a value you can use, e.g.

    $mashed_x = mashup($x)

String functions

ctype_alnum($str) Returns TRUE if $str contains *only* alphanumeric characters.

ctype_alpha($str) Returns TRUE if $str contains *only* alphabetic characters.

ctype_digit($str) Returns TRUE if $str contains *only* numeric characters. Unlike is_numeric(), this will return FALSE if $str has a decimal point in it.

html_entity_decode($str) Performs the reverse of htmlentities($str).

htmlentities($str) Replaces certain characters with their equivalent HTML entities – e.g. < becomes < which can be useful if you want to display code snippets on screen without them being processed.

is_numeric($str) Returns TRUE if $str can be handled as a number.

nl2br($str) Replaces new lines in $str with HTML <BR/> tags – useful for displaying long text items input from a TEXTAREA.

str_ireplace($x, $y, $str) Searches $str for $x, and replaces it with $y wherever it occurs. All three can be arrays, so you can search and replace multiple terms in multiple strings. NOT case-sensitive.

str_replace($x, $y, $str) As above, only the search is case-sensitive.

strip_tags($str) Removes HTML and PHP tags from $str (a useful security precaution against hackers trying to insert potentially harmful material into your pages).

stripos($str, $x) Searches $str and returns the first occurrence of $x as a number (the *n*th character of $str). If $x is not found in $str, the function returns FALSE. NOT case-sensitive.

stripslashes($str)   Removes backslashes before single and double quotes in **$str**, and replaces double backslashes with single ones – useful for displaying strings which had slashes automatically added.

strlen($str)   Returns the number of characters in the string **$str**.

strpos($str, $x)   Searches **$str** and returns the first occurrence of **$x** as a number (the *n*th character of **$str**). If **$x** is not found in **$str**, the function returns FALSE. Case-sensitive.

strripos($str, $x)   Searches **$str** and returns the *last* occurrence of **$x** as a number. NOT case-sensitive.

strrpos($str, $x)   As above, only the search is case-sensitive.

strtolower($str)   Converts all characters in **$str** to lower case.

strtoupper($str)   Converts all characters in **$str** to upper case.

substr($str, $n, $x)   Returns a substring of length $x characters, starting at the $*n*th character of **$str**.

trim($str)   Removes spaces from both ends of **$str**.

Mathematical functions

acos($x)   Returns the arc cosine of **$x**.

asin($x)   Returns the arc sine of **$x**.

atan($x)   Returns the arc tangent of **$x**.

cos($x)   Returns the cosine of **$x**.

dechex($x)   Converts the decimal number **$x** to its hexadecimal equivalent.

exp($x)   Raises **e** to the power of **$x**.

hexdec($x)   Converts the hexadecimal number **$x** to its decimal equivalent.

log($x)   Returns the natural log of **$x**.

log10($x)   Returns the base-10 log of **$x**.

pow($x, $n)   Raises $x to the power of $n.

round($x, $d)   Takes $x and rounds it up or down to $d decimal places.

sin($x)   Returns the sine of $x.

sqrt($x)   Returns the square root of $x.

tan($x)   Returns the tangent of $x.

MySQL functions

If you have come across PHP's MySQL functions in the past, the extra 'i's in the function names (e.g. mysqli_connect() instead of mysql_connect) may be confusing.

The standard suite of functions for working with MySQL databases has been upgraded to take advantage of the new features available as of MySQL 4.1.3. These new functions are to avoid problems of backwards compatibility with older versions of MySQL, and are differentiated with an 'i' (for 'Improved').

If you are working with a version of MySQL earlier than 4.1.3 you should use the old functions. In many cases this just means removing the 'i' from the function names below, but be aware that some functions take different parameters.

For instance, the new connection function mysqli_connect() takes four parameters: $host, $user, $pass, and $db. The old function mysql_connect() only takes the first three of these, and then has a separate function mysqli_select_db() for choosing a database to work with.

mysqli_connect($host, $user, $pass, $db)   Attempts to open a connection to the MySQL database $db on the server $host, with username $user and password $pass.

mysqli_query($link, $query)   Performs the query $query on the selected database, using the connection $link.

mysqli_fetch_array($result)   Analyses the $result object returned by a query, and returns the first row as an associative array with the column name as the index and the field contents as the value.

mysqli_num_rows($result)   Returns the number of records contained in the results object $result.

`mysqli_affected_rows($link)` Returns the number of records affected by the last `INSERT` or `UPDATE` query executed via the connection `$link`. It will return -1 if the query was invalid.

`mysqli_insert_id($link)` Returns the ID number that was auto-generated by the last `INSERT` query executed via the connection `$link`. If there is no column with an `AUTO_INCREMENT` set, the function will return zero.

`mysqli_error($link)` Returns a description of the last error encountered by MySQL on the connection `$link`.

`mysqli_close($link)` Closes the connection `$link`.

13.4 Online resources

Official software sites, manuals, FAQs and other Help

http://www.php.net The official PHP site, where you will find news, downloads, documentation and more.

http://www.php.net/manual/en The PHP manual online (English versions).

http://www.phpbuilder.com/board Message board at PHPBuilder.com – an active board with lots of useful advice, for all levels of PHP user.

http://www.mysql.com The official MySQL site, where you will find news, downloads, documentation and more.

http://dev.mysql.com/doc/mysql/en/ The MySQL manual online (English versions).

http://www.mysqlfront.de MySQL Front is a nice front-end tool to administer MySQL databases without having to use the command line.

http://asp2php.naken.cc ASP2PHP is a program which takes pages written in ASP (mainly VBScript) and converts them to PHP.

Web hosts offering good PHP/MySQL deals

http://www.titaninternet.co.uk   Titan Internet are a competent, friendly and flexible hosting company with good rates and excellent service. Highly recommended.

http://www.positive-internet.com   Another great value host with top service. Positive Internet are open-source specialists (they have no Windows servers at all) so are very PHP-friendly.

http://webhosting.lycos.co.uk   Lycos is a big player in Europe, offering very cheap off-the-rack PHP/MySQL web space. If you are happy with a standard package and don't care about the personal touch, this could be a bargain.

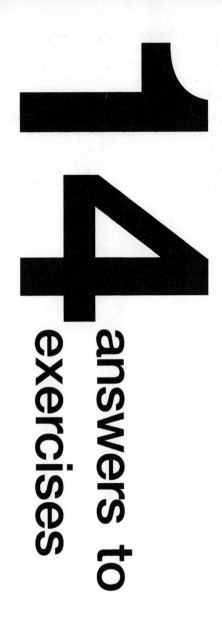

14 answers to exercises

Chapter 2

Q2

```
<HTML>
<BODY>
I am a <? echo "<b>bold adventurer</b> " ; ?>
into the world of <? echo "<i>PHP programming</i>."
; ?>
</BODY>
</HTML>
```

Q3

```
<BODY BGCOLOR="<? echo "#DA3799" ; ?>">
```

Chapter 3

Q1

```
<?
$str1 = "He said" ;
$str2 = "\"Julie baby," ;
$str2 .= " You're my flame\"" ;
$str3 = $str1 . " " . $str2 ;
echo $str3 ;
?>
```

Q2

```
<?
$str1 = "You give me fever… fever that's so hard to
bear" ;
$substr1 = substr($str1, 12, 8) ;
$substr2 = substr($str1, 27, 9) ;
echo $substr1 . "<br/>" ;
echo $substr2 ;
?>
```

Q3

```
  <?
$num = 21 ;
$pcent = $num/42 * 100 ;
echo $num . " as % of 42 is: " . $pcent . "<br/>";
$sqr = ($num * $num) + ($num/2) ;
```

```
echo $num . " squared plus half itself is: " . $sqr
. "<br/>";
$$sqrt = $num - M_SQRT2 ;
echo $num . " minus root 2 is: " . $sqrt;
?>
```

Chapter 4

Q1

```
<?
$lang = "Spanish" ;
if ($lang == "French") {
     $msg = "Salut mon vieux." ;
} elseif ($lang == "Spanish") {
     $msg = "Hola compadre" ;
} else {
     $msg = "Hello old bean." ;
}
echo $msg ;
?>
```

Q2

```
<?
$beans = TRUE ;
$garlic = TRUE ;
$parsnips = TRUE ;
if ($parsnips == TRUE) {
   $msg = "Yuk!" ;
} else {
   if ($garlic == TRUE) {
      $msg = "Mmm, delicious!" ;
   } else {
      if ($beans == TRUE) {
         $msg = "Quite tasty." ;
      } else {
         $msg = "No special ingredients." ;
      }
   }
}
echo $msg ;
?>
```

Q3

```
<?
for ($i=99; $i>0; $i-) {
   echo "$i bottles of beer on the wall, " ;
echo "$i bottles of beer.<br/>" ;
echo "Take one down, pass it around, " ;
echo "($i-1) bottles of beer on the wall…<br/>" ;
}
?>
```

Q4

```
<?
$s1 = $s2 = "s" ;
for ($i=99; $i>0; $i-) {
   if ($i==1) {
      $s1 = "" ;
      $s2 = "s" ;
   } elseif ($i==2) {
      $s2 = "" ;
   }
   echo "$i bottle$s1 of beer on the wall, " ;
   echo "$i bottle$s1 of beer.<br/>" ;
   echo "Take one down, pass it around, " ;
   echo ($i-1) . " bottle$s2 of beer on the
wall...<p>" ;
}
?>
```

Chapter 5

Q1

Howdy. If you like this page, you can <A HREF="<?
echo $_SERVER['PHP_SELF'] ; ?>">click here</A> to
see it again!
If not, just <A HREF="<? echo
$_SERVER['HTTP_REFERER'] ; ?>">click here</A> to go
back to where you were!

Q2

Howdy. If you like this page, you can <A HREF="<?
echo $_SERVER['PHP_SELF'] ; ?>">click here</A> to

```
see it again!
<?
if (array_key_exists('HTTP_REFERER', $_SERVER)) {
   $ref = $_SERVER['HTTP_REFERER'] ;
   echo "<p>If not, <A HREF=\"$ref\">click here</A>
to go back to where you were." ;
}
?>
```

Q3

```
<HEAD>
<? $css = (array_key_exists('css', $_GET) ?
$_GET['css'] : "default") ; ?>
<LINK REL="stylesheet" TYPE="text/css" HREF="<?
echo $css ?>.css"/>
</HEAD>
<BODY>
<P><A HREF="<? echo $_SERVER['PHP_SELF'] ?>">
Default stylesheet</a><BR/>
<A HREF="<? echo $_SERVER['PHP_SELF']
?>?css=css1">First stylesheet</a><BR/>
<A HREF="<? echo $_SERVER['PHP_SELF']
?>?css=css2">Second stylesheet</a></P>
```

Chapter 6

Q2

```
<HEAD>
<?
include 'answer0602a.php' ;
$widget = array_key_exists('widget', $_GET) ?
$_GET['widget'] : "gizmo" ;

function apply_style($widget) {
   $style = $widget[1] . ".css" ;
   echo "<LINK REL=\"stylesheet\" TYPE=\"text/css\"
HREF=\"$style\"/>" ;
}

function describe_widget($widget) {
   echo "<B>Widget name:</B> $widget[0]<BR/>" ;
```

```
      echo "<B>Category:</B> $widget[1]" ;
      echo "<P>This device $widget[2]." ;
}

apply_style($$widget) ;
?>
</HEAD>
<BODY>
<? describe_widget($$widget) ; ?>
</BODY>
```

Q3

```
function delivery_cost($widget) {
echo "<B>Price:</B> &euro;$widget[3] plus " ;
   if ($widget[4] <= 1) {
      return "free delivery" ;
   } else {
      return "&euro;" . (($widget[4]-1)*15.25) . "
shipping costs." ;
   }
}
```

Chapter 7

There is not enough space here to show sample answer code in full, but the following pseudocode should give you some pointers for all three exercises.

```
<?
// set up default values, e.g. empty form error
// flags, prices per day on each vehicle, welcome
// message, etc
$name_err = $tel_err = $email_err = "";
$error_flag = " STYLE='background-color: #FFFFAA;'
";
$price_extras = array("aircon" => 35, "cd" => 25);
$intro = "Welcome..."; // etc.

// if posted, process the form
if ($_POST) {
   // assign values from form
   $name = $_POST['name']; // etc...
```

```php
    // conditional expression so vehicle/hire details
    // are NOT processed if this is a reset (Ex.3)
    if (!IsSet($_POST['reset'])) {
        $veh = $_POST['veh']; // etc...

        // check for extras (if none submitted, array
        // index will be undefined)
        if (IsSet($_POST['extra_aircon']))
        $extra_aircon = $_POST['extra_aircon']; //etc.

        // check for mandatory fields (Ex.2)
        if ($name == "") {
            $name_err = $error_flag;
            $error .= "<BR/>Please enter your name." ;
        } // etc...

        // validate period is integer (Ex.2)
        } elseif (!ctype_digit($period)) {
            $period_err = $error_flag;
            $error .= "<BR>Please enter a whole number
of days for the duration of hire.";
        }

        // assign drop-down SELECTED values (Ex.2)
        if ($veh != "") {
            if ($veh == "lambo") $veh_lambo = "SELECTED";
    // etc...
        }

        // checkboxes are assigned CHECKED values from
        // form values
        // validate email address (Ex.2 - see p.105
        // for this code)
        // clean telephone number (see p.104)

        // if no errors, calculate quote
        if ($error == "") {
            $price = ($price_per_day[$veh] * $period) +
        $extra_costs;
            $intro = "Thank you. Based on your
    . requirements, the cost of your vehicle rental
    will be £$price.";
```

```
    } else {
        $intro = "Sorry, we need a little more
information to complete the quotation process.";
    }
  }
}
echo "$intro <BR/>";

// if not posted, or if posted with errors (Ex.2),
// or if this is a reset (Ex.3), display form
if ( (!$_POST) || ($error != "") ||
(IsSet($_POST['reset'])) ) {
?>

<SPAN STYLE="color: red; font-weight: bold;"><?
echo $error; ?></SPAN>

<FORM METHOD="POST" ACTION="<? $_SERVER['PHP_SELF']
?>">
<TABLE>
 <TR>
   <TD <? echo $name_err ?> ><B>Name:</B></TD>
   <TD COLSPAN="3" <? echo $name_err ?> ><INPUT
TYPE="text" NAME="name" VALUE="<? echo $name ?>"
SIZE="75" /></TD>
 </TR>
<!-- etc... -->
 <TR>
   <TD VALIGN="top" <? echo $veh_err ?> >
   <B>Vehicle:</B></TD>
   <TD VALIGN="top" <? echo $veh_err ?> ><SELECT
NAME="veh">
     <OPTION VALUE="">Please select...</OPTION>
     <OPTION VALUE="lambo" <? echo $veh_lambo ?> >
   Lamborghini Murcielago</OPTION>
     <!- etc... ->
   </SELECT></TD>
   <TD VALIGN="top"><B>Extras:</B></TD>
   <TD><INPUT TYPE="checkbox" NAME="extra_aircon"
VALUE="CHECKED" <? echo $extra_aircon ?> /> Air
con<BR/>
   <!-- etc... --></TD>
```

```
  </TR>
<!-- etc... -->
 <TR>
   <TD><INPUT TYPE="submit" VALUE="SUBMIT" /></TD>
   <TD COLSPAN="3"><INPUT TYPE="reset" VALUE=
"CANCEL" /></TD>
 </TR>
</TABLE>
</FORM>

<? // else show link to re-quote (Ex.3)
} else {
?>
   <BR/> <BR/>
   <FORM METHOD="POST" ACTION="<? $_SERVER
      ['PHP_SELF'] ?>">
   <INPUT TYPE="hidden" NAME="reset" VALUE = "1" />
   <INPUT TYPE="hidden" NAME="name" VALUE = "<?
echo $name ?>" />
   <INPUT TYPE="hidden" NAME="tel" VALUE = "<? echo
$tel ?>" />
   <INPUT TYPE="hidden" NAME="email" VALUE = "<?
echo $email ?>" />
   <INPUT TYPE="submit" VALUE="CHANGE REQUIREMENTS" />
   </FORM>
<? // end show / don't show form conditional
}
?>
```

Chapter 8

Q1

```
Cookie-setting page:
<?
// if the form has been sent, store details in a
// cookie
if (IsSet($_POST['name'])) {
   setcookie('name', $_POST['name'], time() + 60);
   setcookie('last_visit', time(), time() + 60);
}
?>
```

```
<HTML>
<HEAD>
<TITLE>The goldfish seducer</TITLE>
</HEAD>
<BODY>
<?
// if the form has not been sent, display it now
if (!IsSet($_POST['name'])) {
?>
   <H2>Please, introduce yourself</H2>
   <FORM METHOD="POST" ACTION="<? echo
$_SERVER['PHP_SELF'] ?>">
   By what name should I refer to this vision of
loveliness I see before me?<BR/>
   <INPUT TYPE="text" NAME="name" SIZE="35" />
   <INPUT TYPE="submit" VALUE="Pray tell" />
   </FORM>
<?
// if the form has been sent, respond
} else {
?>
   <H2><? echo $_POST['name'] ?></H2>
   How charming, what a lovely name!<BR/> <BR/>
Please do <A HREF="answer0801a.php">visit me
again</A> some time.
<?
// close if...else brackets
}
?>
</BODY>
</HTML>


Cookie-retrieving page:
<HTML>
<HEAD>
<TITLE>The goldfish seducer</TITLE>
</HEAD>
<BODY>
<?
if (IsSet($_COOKIE['last_visit'])) {
   $t_elapsed = time() - $_COOKIE['last_visit'];
} else {
```

```
      $t_elapsed = 0;
}
if (!IsSet($_COOKIE['name'])) {
   print "<H2>Well hell-ooooo...</H2>";
   print "I don't believe I've seen you around here
before. ";
   print "Why don't you come in and <A
   HREF='answer0801.php'>introduce yourself</A>?";
} else {
   print "<H2>You're back!</H2>";
   print "Oh my sweet " . $_COOKIE['name'] . "!
It's been so long! ";
   if ($t_elapsed != 0) {
      echo "($t_elapsed seconds to be exact)";
   }
}
?>
</BODY>
</HTML>
```

Q2/3

```
<?
session_start();

$questions = array(
   1 => "What is your quest?",
   2 => "What is your favourite colour?",
   3 => "What is the airspeed velocity of an un-
laden swallow?");

$answers = array(
   1 => "Holy Grail",
   2 => "blue",
   3 => "African or European swallow");

// set default intro text
$intro = "Stop! Who would cross the Bridge of Death
must answer me<BR/>these questions three, ere the
other side ye'll see...";

// if this is the first Q or if the quiz has been
// reset, start counting and scoring
```

```php
if ( (!IsSet($_SESSION['q_num'])) ||
(IsSet($_POST['retry'])) ) {
   $q_num = $_SESSION['q_num'] = 0;
   $score = $_SESSION['score'] = 0;
// otherwise, add one to last count if answer
// received
} else {
   $q_num = $_SESSION['q_num'] = $_SESSION['q_num']
+ 1;
}
// if form submitted (and q_num <= 3), process  //
answer
if ( (IsSet($_POST['answer'])) && ($q_num <= 3) ) {

   // answer is right if it contains the
   // corresponding element in the $answers array
   if (stripos($_POST['answer'], $answers[$q_num])
!== FALSE) {
      $_SESSION['score'] = $score =
   $_SESSION['score'] + 1;
      $intro = "Well done, brave sir knight!";
   } else {
      $score = $_SESSION['score'];
      $intro = "Nay, foolish knight!";
   }
   $intro .= " Your score so far is $score.";

   // if last question, decide pass or fail
   if ($q_num == 3) {
      if ($score == 3) {
         $intro = "What? I... I don't know that...
      AAAAAGGGGHHHHH!<BR/> <BR/>[Well done, you
      succeeded and may cross the Bridge of Death]";
      } else {
         $intro = "AAAAAGGGGHHHHH! [You failed and
      are flung into the gorge]";
      }
   }
}
?>
<HTML>
```

```
<BODY>
<H2>Quest Quiz</H2>

<?
echo $intro . "<BR/> <BR/>";
// show question form as long as the quiz is not
// finished
if ($q_num < 3) {
?>

<FORM METHOD="POST" ACTION="<? $_SERVER['PHP_SELF']
?>">
   Q<? echo ($q_num + 1) ?>.
<? echo $questions[($q_num + 1)] ?><BR/>
   <INPUT TYPE="text" NAME="answer" SIZE="35" />
   <INPUT TYPE="submit" VALUE="SUBMIT" />
</FORM>

<?
// otherwise show cookie-resetting form
} else {
?>

<FORM METHOD="POST" ACTION="<? $_SERVER['PHP_SELF']
?>">
   <INPUT TYPE="hidden" NAME="retry" VALUE="1" />
   <INPUT TYPE="submit" VALUE="START AGAIN" />
</FORM>

<? } ?>
</BODY>
</HTML>
```

Chapter 10

Q1

```
CREATE TABLE products (
id SMALLINT UNSIGNED PRIMARY KEY AUTO_INCREMENT,
name VARCHAR(127),
description VARCHAR(127),
price DECIMAL(5,2),
```

qty_avail MEDIUMINT UNSIGNED DEFAULT 0,
instructions MEDIUMTEXT DEFAULT 'No instructions
supplied');

Q2

INSERT INTO products (name, description, price,
qty_avail)
    VALUES ('doodah', 'A thingummy which screws onto
the wotsit to stop the knick-knack falling off',
9.99, 5);

Q3

SELECT id, name, price FROM products
(a) WHERE price < 9.99;
(b) WHERE description LIKE '%screw%';

Q4

UPDATE products SET price = (price - price * 0.15)
WHERE price < 15;

$_COOKIE **122**, **191**
$_COOKIES **72**
$_GET **71**, **191**
$_POST **72**, **191**
$_REQUEST **72**, **191**
$_SERVER **67**
$_SESSION **125**, **191**
.NET **180**

acos( ) **195**
ADD **150**
ADODB objects **187**
ALTER TABLE **149**
AND operator (&&) **55**
Apache and PHP, configuring **21**
Apache web server, installation **15**
Arguments **90**
Array index **47**
Array( ) function **46**
Arrays **46**
  as arguments **91**
  using data from **63**
asin( ) **195**
ASP **180**
ASP2PHP **181**
  optional flags **185**
  using **184**
atan( ) **195**
AUTO_INCREMENT **149**

BIGINT **147**
Boolean variables **57**
Browsers **67**

CHANGE **150**
CHAR(N) **147**
Client-side **3**
Code and content, keeping apart
  172
Column types **145**
Column types (MySQL)
  date/time **147**
  numeric **146**
  string **147**
Comments **43**
Comparison operators **51**, **192**
Concatenation **41**
Constants **31**
Control structures **50**
  debugging **60**
Cookies **72**, **117**
  deleting **123**
  editing **123**
  expiry **118**
  multiple **123**
  retrieving **122**
  using **119**
cos( ) **195**
CREATE DATABASE **144**
CREATE TABLE **148**
ctype_alnum( ) **103**, **194**
ctype_alpha( ) **103**, **194**
ctype_digit( ) **103**, **194**

Data, validating **101**
Data types **142**

Databases **141**
  design **141**
  indexing **142**
  inputting data **167**
  names **145**
  records **150**
DATE **147**
DATETIME **147**
Debugging control structures **60**
dechex( ) **195**
DECIMAL(P,S) **147**
DEFAULT **149**
DELETE FROM **155**
DESCRIBE **149**
Do… While… **60**
DROP **149**

echo **26**, **35**, **193**
Elseif **53**
EOF (End Of File) **41**
Error-trapping **74**, **127**
Escape characters **36**
exp( ) **195**
EXPIRE **118**

Files, included **82**
Firewalls **135**
Flowchart **57**
For… **63**
Foreach… **63**
Form data **72**
  cleaning **103**
Form reset buttons **114**
Forms
  error messages **111**
  processing **99**, **108**
Functions **81**
  calling **92**
  defining **90**
  user-defined **91**
  with default values **94**

Heredoc **41**
hexdec( ) **195**
Hidden fields **101**
HTML, outputting **37**
html_entity_decode( ) **102**, **194**
htmlentities( ) **102**, **194**

HTTP **117**
HTTP header **120**
HTTP_ACCEPT_LANGUAGE
    68, **190**
HTTP_REFERER **68**, **190**
HTTP_USER_AGENT **68**, **190**

If… Else… **52**
If… Elself… Else… **53**
IIS (Internet Information Services)
    12
Improved MySQL **137**
include **81**, **193**
include_once **193**
Included files **82**
Infinite loops **61**
INSERT **167**
INT **146**
is_numeric( ) **103**, **194**
Iteration **50**

Just if… **54**

LAMP **13**
Lerdorf, Rasmus **3**
LIKE operator **153**
log( ) **195**
log10( ) **195**
LONGTEXT **147**

Mathematical functions **195**
Mathematical operators **192**
Maths **43**
  in MySQL **154**
Maths constants **46**
MD5 checksum **14**, **132**
MEDIUMINT **146**
MEDIUMTEXT **147**
mmysqli_close( ) **158**
MODIFY **150**
MySQL
  configuration **133**
  connecting to from PHP **158**
  download **131**
  history of **5**
  installation **132**
  maths **154**
  working with **137**

MySQL command line **135, 137, 144**
MySQL functions **196**
MySQL(i) **188**
MySQL-Front **138**
mysqli_affected_rows( ) **197**
mysqli_close( ) **197**
mysqli_connect( ) **158, 196**
mysqli_error( ) **197**
mysqli_fetch_array( ) **161, 196**
mysqli_insert_id( ) **197**
mysqli_num_rows( ) **196**
mysqli_query( ) **160, 196**

Nested If structures **56**
nl2br( ) **102, 194**
NOT NULL **149**
Numeric expressions, order of evaluation **43**
Numeric variables **33, 44**

Operating systems **12**
OR operator (||) **55**
ORDER BY **164**
Output and script functions **193**
Outputting HTML **37**

Perl **3**
PHP
  and forms **98**
  embedding in HTML **26**
  history of **3**
  installation, troubleshooting **24**
  installing for use with Apache **18**
  installing for use with Microsoft IIS **22**
  possible applications **8**
  reasons to use **5**
  to write HTML tags **27**
PHP 5, configuring with MySQL **136**
PHP and MySQL, usage **7**
PHP engine **12**
PHP functions **193**
PHP operators **191**
PHP_SELF **68, 190**
PRIMARY KEY **149**
pow( ) **196**

Primary keys **142**
print **193**
Privacy **118**

Query string, information from **72**
QUERY_STRING **190**

Records
  deleting **154**
  displaying one **161**
  displaying in table **163**
  displaying multiple **162**
  extracting **160**
  filtering **153, 165**
  inserting **167**
  modifying **153**
  sorting **164**
  updating **170**
require **193**
Results object **160**
return **194**
round( ) **196**

SCRIPT_FILENAME **190**
SELECT **143, 151, 160**
Server side includes **82**
Server-side **3**
Server-side scripting **8**
SERVER_NAME **68, 190**
Session variables **117, 118**
  setting and retrieving **126**
  using **125**
session_start( ) **125**
setcookie( ) **120**
sin( ) **196**
SMALLINT **146**
Software, verifying **13, 132**
SQL **5, 143**
SQL queries **160**
SQL syntax **143**
str_ireplace( ) **103, 194**
str_replace( ) **103, 194**
String and assignment operators **191**
String functions **102, 194**
String variables **33**
Strings **41**
strip_tags( ) **103, 194**

stripos( ) **103**, **194**
stripslashes( ) **103**, **195**
strlen( ) **102**, **195**
strpos( ) **103**, **195**
strripos( ) **103**, **195**
strrpos( ) **103**, **195**
strtolower( ) **195**
strtoupper( ) **102**, **195**
Structured Query Language **5**
Substrings **42**
Superglobal arrays **190**
    $_COOKIE **122**
    $_SESSION **125**

Tables
    altering **149**
    creating with SQL **148**
    names **145**
tan( ) **196**
Ternary operator **53**
TEXT **147**
TIME **147**
TIMESTAMP **147**
TINYINT **146**
TINYTEXT **147**
trim( ) **102**, **195**
True and false **51**

Truth conditions **51**
    complex **55**

Unix timestamp **121**
UNSIGNED **149**
UPDATE **154**, **167**
USE **144**

Validation **106**
Values **30**
VARCHAR(N) **147**
Variable includes **88**
Variable variables **92**
Variables **30**
    defining **32**
    predefined **190**
    recognizing **31**
    rules for names **33**
    types **33**
VBScript **181**

WAMP **12**
Web hosting **137**
Web server **12**
While… **60**

YEAR **147**